MW01592979

Laughing All the Way

Not Your Usual Breast Cancer Journal

Juliana M. Steele

All rights reserved. No part of this book may be reproduced by any mechanical, photographic or electronic process, or in the form of phonographic recording; nor may it be stored in a retrieval system, transmitted or otherwise be copied for public or private use - other than for "fair use" as brief quotations embodied in articles and reviews - without prior written permission by the author.

The author of this book does not dispense medical advice. This book is her personal experience with breast cancer and her own thoughts on the experiences she had with the treatment prescribed for her by her doctor. She does not specifically prescribe or advocate the use of any technique or treatment she underwent for any physical, emotional, or medical problem. That is between you and your doctor. In the event that you use any of the information in this book for yourself, which is your constitutional right, the author and publisher assume no responsibility for your actions.

Photo cover credit - my husband, Kenneth H. Johnson

Proofreading – Claudette Cruz, The Editing Sweetheart

Copyright © 2019 Juliana M. Steele

All rights reserved.

FIRST EDITION

ISBN:
ISBN-978-0-9859513-3-7 print

DEDICATION

For my husband, Ken Johnson. Without his unwavering love, support, and encouragement, lemons would just be lemons.

Contents

Laughing All the Way

ACKNOWLEDGMENTS

I would like to thank:

Dr. Regan Rostorfer, my oncologist at Orlando Health, whose never-ending patience and willingness to explain the intricate nuances of all aspects of my treatment made him the consummate tour guide for my adventure. In his capable hands, all things are possible.

Dr. Jeffery Smith, my surgeon at Orlando Health, who took the time to listen to me and understand who I was and what was important to me and implement that as best as he could during surgery. I am ecstatic with the results and will be forever grateful that I ended up in his skilled hands.

Dr. Tomas Dvorak, my radiation oncologist, whose patience and willingness to explain the process of radiation therapy and how it affects every layer of tissue it will come in contact with was not only educational, but honored me as a patient. I thank you for that and am grateful to have had you on my team.

Dr. Diane Robinson in the Integrative Medicine/Cancer Support Community, who understands that while illness strikes the body, treatment and care must embrace the whole person.

Valerie Kelley, artist-in-residence at Orlando Health, for the amazing art therapy work she does with patients throughout the hospital. Never underestimate the healing power of unleashed creativity.

Laura Martin, my breast care center navigator. Without you, I would be lost.

The myriad of nurses, technicians, phlebotomists, insurance specialists, check-in specialists, research specialists, volunteers, and on and on and on, who make Orlando Health the amazing hospital it is. Without your professionalism and ready smiles, Orlando Health would be just another hospital.

Connie, Sammy, and everyone who read my blog and followed along as the adventure unfolded. Your encouragement was priceless.

And the Archangel Gabriel, without whose encouragement this book would never be.

Introduction

This book jumps right in, so some context may be helpful. In June of 2016, I was diagnosed with breast cancer. I have a large family, so to keep everyone apprised of what was going on, I started a blog. Little did I know that it would find its way around the world, touching lives as it went. This book was created from that blog.

While my adventure was with breast cancer, we all face life events that give us pause. This book transcends the malady that prompted it and is a celebration of how to embrace life, no matter what your situation, and live the heck out of it. I did, and so can you.

If you read my blog and followed along as I lived the events on these pages, thank you for your support. By reading about me, your energy joined the thousands of others that read along and made a difference.

If this book found you, then you are now part of the family. Read it, enjoy it, share it. I never know what chapter resonates with whom, but there is something in here for everyone.

I include a lot of tips, so for those with paperback versions there is a Notes page at the end. For those with e-books, you have bookmarks.

Thank you again, and enjoy!

Juliana M. Steele

Chapter 1 - I'm Happy, Really, Really Happy. Oh, and I Have Breast Cancer

I'm happy. Really, I'm very, very happy. Oh, and I have stage III breast cancer. And I'm happy, really, really happy.

To catch you up on the last three months -

End of June 2016 - Ultrasound and mammogram showed calcification that had obviously gone on a growing binge. This did generate a little stress, but denial is a delightful panacea.

August 2016 - Breast biopsy confirmed invasive ductal carcinoma. The word *carcinoma* is really an ugly word. They should come up with a more optimistic word for cancer, one that is not so harsh and threatening sounding. Linguistically, invasive ductal carcinoma rolls off the tongue and plummets to the floor, taking your psyche, confidence and ain't-it-a-glorious-day attitude with it. (Not to worry, they can be retrieved, dusted off, and reinstated.) A more empathetic-sounding diagnosis would leave some of that intact, and you would be more likely to actually hear what the doctor says after that.

For the record, a breast biopsy hurts like hell and continues to hurt like hell for the better part of a month. The doctor will tell you otherwise, but don't buy it. The truth is it hurts, it will heal, and you will have moved on to something else long before the latter, so it will become moot in short order, but it still hurts like hell when you are going through it. Knowing that will ease the disappointment when all of a sudden you realize it's not the kind of test you walk away from as if nothing happened. One disclaimer here, the pain is as much psychological as it is physical. It is the only appointment I cried after. I managed to keep it together until I got out the door and then I cried great gut-wrenching sobs on the front steps of the Women's Center for Radiology.

Back to the timeline ... next came meeting after meeting with surgeons, oncologists, radiation therapists, plastic surgeons. Interviewing doctors is no different than interviewing for any position in your life. If you don't click and it's not a good fit, you keep looking.

Creep forward to September 2016, and I am having an ultrasound of my lymph nodes. One looks irregular. Another biopsy. Not as bad as the breast biopsy, but they did clip a nerve so now the area of skin where my pectoral muscle meets my left arm has a perpetual feeling of sunburned tenderness. On Friday, September 30, 2016, I had the last of a three-month string of tests. A PET scan. Good news, the cancer is localized in my left breast and there is no indication of cancer anywhere else. Five days later, on October 5, I had my first chemo session.

Some things I've learned so far -

Life Lesson #1 - YOU ARE IN CHARGE! If you don't like a doctor, or a hospital as was the case with me, GET ANOTHER ONE. You are going to spend A LOT of time with these folks, so it is important that you respect them and trust them, as it will literally be with your life.

Life Lesson #2 - All that matters is today and tomorrow. Don't think too far down the road. It will make you crazy and it will likely not play out the way you want it to, anyway. I spent the first month trying to plan out how my treatments were going to fall, attempting to puzzle them in among work, hobbies, my life. Don't. Your life isn't your work or your hobbies or what you do. Your life is YOU. Mine hasn't changed in terms of what I do, but it has changed in terms of the amount of time I allocate to each of those things and the amount of time I spend on **ME**. Remember, you are not what you do. **YOU ARE YOU**. Pay attention to yourself!

Life Lesson #3 - Attitude really is everything. Find humor and wonder in anything and everything you can. I consider this foray into breast cancer an *adventure*. My port is my *alien friend*. The hospital that I am being treated at I call the *Orlando Health Spa*. Really, it's not far off. It is a state-of-the-art facility with a renowned Cancer Center. Every time I go there, I leave happy, no matter what is on the agenda. So why not embrace the adventure, enjoy my days at the spa, and be grateful for the strange alien that has taken up residence on the right side of my chest? There is always an upside, you just have to find it and run with it.

I am happy. Having breast cancer does not define me. I define me. I am the same person, with a slightly more advantageous perspective and a lot more bliss flowing through my veins. Trust me, there is room enough for chemo and bliss, and they don't cancel one another out.

Juliana M. Steele

CHEMOTHERAPY

Chapter 2 - My First Chemo Day and the Butterfly Effect

For me, my first chemo day was pretty uneventful. All the nurses at the UF Health Cancer Center are exceptionally nice, and they were happy to explain anything and everything to me about the process as many times as I needed them to. In terms of the day itself, the first thing that happens is blood work, so off I went to the blood-draw station. In the blood-draw station they took my vitals—blood pressure, temperature, oxygen saturation, etc.— and made sure I was indeed me (wrist band check!), then took me over to the port nurse to have my "port accessed" (it sounds worse than it is). The nurse sterilizes the port area and then sticks a needle into the port with several IV tubes attached to it. Since my port is right at the surface of the skin, the needle was short and I didn't feel a thing. (The lidocaine cream I generously slathered over the site before I left home helped on that front, too.) Then she took blood for the pre-chemo blood work and I was parked in the chemo lounge to wait for the results of the blood work.

I'm not a fan of needles or seeing my own blood in tubes, but I managed to walk from the blood-draw station to my chemo lounge with an IV line hanging off my chest without passing out, so I'm pretty proud of myself for that. With that small victory under my belt, I'm working on changing the narrative I tell myself about needles and blood work. Just because I've had poor experiences in the past doesn't mean I can't have good ones going forward. So far, so good!

The pre-chemo blood work is an important part of each session. Nothing happens after that until the lab work from the blood draw comes back, giving you the green light for chemo. It tells your doctor whether or not you have rebounded from the first session and are okay to proceed. They check your organ functions and blood counts. I have to say, it does give me a good feeling that they are so particular about everything.

Once my blood work was cleared, the order for my chemo was placed. The chemo is prepared on-site in a chemo pharmacy and is special-mixed based on your prescription and weight. Once the chemo was ordered, they started my pre-chemo medications and I had to take a preemptive anti-nausea pill. When my chemo bags were delivered, the chemo nurse brought them over to me and showed me the labels on them to confirm that the name and birthdate on them was mine. I have two drugs for my first phase of chemo: Adriamycin and Cytoxan. One is red and is a fifteen-minute infusion and the other is clear and is a one-hour infusion. I didn't really feel anything while I was being infused (nor are you supposed to). When the bags were done, the chemo nurse flushed the port and removed the needle and I was on my way.

That evening, I didn't know what to expect. I had heard so much about nausea and vomiting that I was on high alert for it to start. I had a light dinner with no problem and went to bed early. I was definitely tired. The day after was the day before Hurricane Matthew. Maybe that added to the surreal nature of the experience. I was waiting to see what would happen in my body and I was waiting to see what would happen outside. I woke up feeling pretty good and did my usual yoga and meditation routine. The most noticeable effects were that I really wasn't hungry, and when I did eat, I felt full quickly, and I was really, really cold. I wasn't nauseous and had no acid reflux (common effects of chemo), so I count myself lucky on that front. The day after chemo, I got a Neulasta shot through a self-injecting gizmo the chemo nurse attached to my arm before I left (after it injects, you just pull it off). The Neulasta stimulates your bone marrow to produce blood cells more quickly.

So here is where the butterfly effect comes in ...

Day 1 - Chemo, afterwards I... was ... tired. And cold. And I stayed cold for pretty much a whole week.

Day 2 - Felt pretty good. I'm thinking that wasn't so bad. I was able to do yoga and meditate without a problem. Neulasta self-injected about 5 p.m.

Day 3 - One long, hazy nap from morning to night. I could barely keep my eyes open for more than half an hour at a time. I have to admit, they were epic naps, the Sunday afternoon snooze on the couch type of naps. Yoga was out of the question, but meditation was blissful.

Day 4 - Woke up at 4 a.m. creaky from the Neulasta shot, so I took an Allegra for the bone ache (an effect of the Neulasta—bone pain). Not as tired, but I ran out of steam early in the evening and slept later than I usually do. Yoga was downgraded to stretching.

Day 5 and 6 - On the mend and able to do some yoga, although my stamina has definitely taken a beating. Meditation cleared the air.

Day 7 - Starting to feel achy all over, like I have the flu, but with no fever or actual flu. I run out of breath easily when I do yoga, so downgraded to stretching and meditation again.

Day 8-9 - Still achy and in flu-less flu mode. Skipped yoga and went straight to meditation.

Day 10 - Ta-da! The butterfly is born! I'm back to full yoga strength and stamina. It's like someone hit a reset button and the pre-chemo me is back.

The main post-chemo effects I had (aside from the fact that toxic substances were coursing through my veins, killing cells) were:

1 - Being cold. And I mean **cold**. Our house is eighty degrees and I slept with two blankets. At one point I even pulled out my flannel pajamas. Chemo makes you cold!

2 - Lack of appetite. Your brain tells you that you need to eat, but your stomach tells you that you are really full. The compromise

was I started to eat calorie-dense foods when I wasn't hungry so that less would still be more (the goal during chemo is not to gain or lose weight).

3 - Some days you just plain hurt. I found it helpful to know it was part of the process and had a finite shelf life. The muscle ache was no worse than the day after an intense workout at the gym, and the flu-like symptoms were definitely better than actually having the flu.

4 - Being tired. I decided to just go with it. I went to bed when I was tired and gave myself a break during the times I felt physically weak. Yoga can take many forms, so I embraced the days when my routine could take a new path.

My next round of chemo is Thursday, October 20, 2016. Oddly, I am actually looking forward to it. I'm curious by nature, so I am eager to compare round I to round II. That, and the end goal of all this remains the same: disrupt the cancer!

Chapter 3 - Finding Peace

One of the most amazing things I have found with cancer is peace. It wasn't easy, and there was a time when I thought it was impossible, but it has come. Looking back, I now know the path of peace has been available to me throughout my whole life, I just chose to take the path of strife, angst, anxiety, and tension instead. There is a path of peace, readily available, for each and every one of us. It is up to each of us to find it, and choose it.

The path of peace is different for all of us. The key is to not bring judgment to the process. Connect in a way that is right for you. In the end, it is whatever brings a peaceful calm over your being that will remain even in the face of adversity.

When I was diagnosed with cancer, the first thing I did was go to the Cassadaga Spiritualist Camp in Cassadaga, Florida (http://www.cassadaga.org). Being of Unitarian roots, I am open to all faiths and paths to spirituality, and the folks at Cassadaga resonate with me. Established in 1894, the "camp" is a community of fifty-five residences of individuals gathered together to practice spiritualism. It is also one of the oldest active religious communities in the United States. Ken and I made a day of it and had tarot card readings, I had a session with a healer, and we poked around the shops.

Tarot card readings can be very enlightening. I think many people get put off by card readings because they want the reader to tell them about themselves, sort of prove they're psychic by reading your mind or something. In reality the cards are speaking directly to you, and the reader is there to guide you to an understanding that only you know the intimate details of. I get much more from readings now that I have let go of my expectation of the reader and instead focus on the messages coming through.

They have a broad range of spiritual practitioners and healers at Cassadaga, so I spent a lot of time reading bios to see who I resonated with, at least on paper. I finally decided on Jackie. She was warm and accepting and we clicked immediately. Having gone in there looking for guidance, I couldn't have had a better experience. The cards said that I was going to have a rough year, but if I did my homework, made the best decisions I could base on what I learned and what was true for me, that I would emerge victorious. Also, I have three archangels looking over me: Gabriel, Michael and Rafael.

After a lunch break, I had a healing session on the crystal bed. The woman who I chose for my healing session was Ayla. She is a druid and works with the earth and moon. I found her immensely fascinating and quite powerful. She did a short reading to see what "toxins" needed clearing and if I had any ancestors that were helping me on this journey, and I was happy to hear that my father is by my side through all of this. The healing bed has large quartz crystals hung over it, each one bathed in the color of the corresponding chakra it hangs above. Ayla did a chanting cleanse and called on the spirits to support me as she laid bags of crystals on each of my chakras, then I was left alone for a twenty-minute meditation. At the end, I came out clear and calm and focused. I knew exactly what my path was and what I had to do to succeed. For me, releasing all the negative energy I have been carrying around my whole life will be key to restoring my health.

To help me stay grounded and focused, I found a wonderful set of tarot cards by Doreen Virtue - *Ascended Masters Oracle.* It is a deck of forty-four cards of male and female deities giving life-affirming messages. Whenever I am feeling uneasy, I pick a card, and I find the messages have always been spot-on and helpful. Guidance so far—meditate, do yoga, encourage joy in my life, embrace peace, connect with nature, and write! As a result, I have embarked on a steady daily routine of slow, mindful yoga (rather than just a yoga workout), followed by a fifteen-minute meditation. I am filling my life with things that inspire me and make me laugh. Things that bring joy and peace. My reading list includes books by David Michie—*The Queen's Corgi, The Dalai Lama's Cat* series, *The Magician of Lhasa*; interspersed with lighthearted books, like Carolyn Brown novels—*The Red-Hot Chili Cook-off,*

The Yellow Rose Beauty Shop and *The PMS Club*; and Dana Moss's *Sweet Taffy and Murder*. In the end, it is whatever works. Judgment aside, go after it. Let it lift you up and carry you onward. Having spent a lifetime doing what I should, now I do what is best for me.

As you can see, what is best for me is nontraditional, mostly eclectic, and definitely free spirited. What works for you may be reconnecting with your faith, meditation may be replaced by prayer (my meditation is a mix of both), your taste in movies and books may take you in a different direction altogether, or you may not read or watch TV at all. It doesn't matter. All that matters is that it works for you. And whatever it is, embrace it, free of judgment, free of second thoughts. It is for you and you alone. Love yourself and go for it!

Chapter 4 - Embracing All Points in Between

In all honesty, it's really not a complete bed of roses to get chemo. Now mid-stream after my second treatment, some things seem new, but in reality I probably just glossed over them the first time. I was so thrilled not to be vomiting uncontrollably that the minor maladies slid by without any real notice. Now, they are under a microscope, so here they are -

1 - My hair fell out. Okay, in all honesty I didn't notice it the first time because it only started falling out after the second round of chemo, but still, one day it's in there as firm as can be and the next you run your fingers through it and come away with a fistful. Me being me, I found it enormously amusing to keep running my fingers through my hair to see if it would abate at all (it didn't), much to the chagrin of my husband. I mean, who wants to watch their wife casually bald themselves one fistful at a time?

2 - The lump in my stomach - it's not really nausea, it's a lump in my stomach. It goes away when I eat, but comes back pretty quickly afterwards. My husband urged me to take the nausea pills they prescribed "as needed." They help a little, but not completely, but then again it's not nausea, it's a lump in my stomach. I don't have a pill for that, but sipping ginger ale fizzes up the situation and gives some reprieve. Lying flat works for a time too.

3 - Dry mouth - when I say dry mouth, I mean DRY MOUTH. I wake up every three hours at night with my mouth so dry, my lips are stuck to my teeth. My nightly routine is: drink water to free my lips, pee, go back to bed. Repeat every three hours, all night. The doctor recommended Biotene Dry Mouth Oral Rinse. It gave me an extra hour before the first hydration cycle, but it also gave my mouth an oily feel. In the end, desperate times may call for desperate measures. If you can't stand the wake-up cycle, give it a go. Me, I just go to bed earlier so I have longer total hours under my belt by morning.

4 - Constipation or diarrhea - I got lucky with the former and have managed to keep it from being an issue through a steady diet of pears (yes, pears are on the same list as prunes in that regard) and other fruits. The more water in your diet the better, and that goes for watery foods.

5 - Changing taste buds - they said my sense of taste would change, but they are changing in a weird way. It's not the taste of things I don't like, it's the consistency. It's like a wire got crossed and the wrong feedback is coming across for the wrong food consistency.

Since I am putting things under a microscope, I should probably add myself. My first round of chemo was pretty mild in terms of effects, and the second round has had some sticking points (see above), but in all fairness, I still have it very easy. I don't have the achiness I had the first go-round, nor do I have the four-day-long headache that accompanied round one. My heart doesn't feel like it's beating a tattoo on the inside of my chest, and the coldness is not as bad. My follow-up visit with the oncologist last Thursday showed my blood had completely rebounded between treatments and the tumor was already shrinking. All in all, I feel blessed. I am under the care of great doctors, I have great friends and family praying for me and rooting for me, and I have a wonderful, loving angel of a husband who is by my side every step of the way. Life is good.

No, I'd like to upgrade that. Life is great!

Chapter 5 - Hair, Hair, Hair, or Not

Losing my hair is another phase of this adventure that I have embraced with gusto. I have been able to do things that I can honestly say were never on my radar before cancer. Let's face it, hair is an accoutrement that most spend a good deal of time on. Men and women alike dye it, perm it, iron it, style it, gel it, mousse it, spray it, braid it, crimp it, adorn it with barrettes and beads and feathers, tame it with headbands and bandannas, and when all that fails, put a wig on or shave it off and go sans. Many spend a lot of time (and money) on their coiffure. I have never been one to embrace that sort of time—or monetary—investment, so when I opted to go the chemo route and looked into why and when my hair would fall out, I embraced it with what has become my hallmark curiosity and sense of adventure. While some of this may sound kooky, it was indeed fun, and I learned a lot.

When I asked at the hospital about the "timing" of hair loss, I was told ten to fourteen days (I later learned it was more like fourteen to twenty-one days). I asked because I had a haircut scheduled for that week and it seemed silly to get a haircut if my hair was going to fall out a week later. So I skipped the haircut and waited. Seven days went by ... ten days went by ... fourteen days went by ... and nothing. So, feeling a bit like Shaggy from *Scooby Doo*, I called my hairdresser (God Bless Jeffrey Spells) and he squeezed me in. I figured I'd go shorter than usual (I keep my hair pretty short anyway), maybe two inches long, with some action on the top. When he washed my hair, Jeffrey broke the news to me—my hair was starting to fall out. Not horribly, but I don't usually lose any hair, so some hair in the sink meant something. I did consider having him shave it off then and there, but thought, nah, I wanted to see how this would play out. Plus, maybe it wouldn't really all fall out. So we went with our original plan.

The haircut lasted one day.

The day after my haircut, my hair was coming out in fistfuls. My husband—who is an angel, by the way—did me a solid and cut it shorter, down to about an inch, with his beard clippers, so I could put a hat on. It didn't take long for me to bear a strong resemblance to a dog with mange. Hair tends to fall out in clumps, it doesn't thin out, so you end up with bald spots. It's one thing to lose your hair, it's another to look, well, mangy. The first night when I took my hat off, the inside was coated with hair. Nope, that wasn't going to work. I didn't mind losing the hair, but I did mind it ending up everywhere. And I mean everywhere—on me, on my clothes, on the bed, on my husband—everywhere.

So it's really falling out. Now is where the fun begins—experimenting with how to get it to fall out faster.

- I tried the shower routine, seeing if I could wash the hair out. It was a disaster. I ended up covered in hair, which is pretty hard to get off you when it is constantly being added to by newly falling-out hair.

- The next thing I tried was to vacuum the hair off my head. Oddly, it worked pretty well, and the vacuum gives an amazing head massage in the process. I used the drapery-cleaning attachment (the round one with the bristles). It works best to have another person do it for you to get the full spa treatment effect. In my case, my husband did it for me. I would be remiss if I did not add—**please do not try this with long hair**. Remember, my hair was short and falling out. Getting live hair that is not falling out tangled inside a vacuum will **NOT** be like a spa treatment. Anyway, the vacuum did get rid of most of the loose hair.

- Clipping it off. Sort of a no-brainer that this one will work. Having my husband do it was extra special. There is something amazingly intimate and loving about having your husband shave your head for you. Plus, he was darn good at it.

So I'm bald, and I actually kind of like it. I mean, in terms of no-fuss hairdos, it doesn't get much more no-fuss than this. I wash my head, slather it with body lotion to keep it soft (Borage, by the way, is awesome stuff), and I'm done. Truth be told, I feel free this way. Suddenly, all those rules of hair etiquette don't apply to me. I have this magical pass to do any crazy thing I want to do to my head, and it's okay. I mean, heck, I vacuumed my head and then shaved it and all of a sudden I've got folks saying I'm brave and strong. If I had done that without having cancer, I doubt those would be the descriptors used. (I do appreciate the encouragement though, so keep it coming!) In the end, it really is just hair, or lack thereof. It doesn't define me, or change me, to have it or not have it. I suppose I would probably feel differently if this was permanent, and who knows, maybe there is a chance it is, but in the end it is an adventure like no other, and I'm going to enjoy the heck out of every moment of it!

Hair firsts -

1 - having my husband shave my head with his beard clippers - twice!

2 - having my head vacuumed (I would do this again, it felt amazing!)

3 - washing my hair and ending up covered in hair (not one I care to repeat)

4 - putting body lotion on my head

Things you cannot do with hair -

1 - enjoy a warm breeze on your scalp (or cool breeze if that is your thing)

2 - run your hand across your head and realize how really, really soft scalp skin is

3 - see the real you, and realize how really, really beautiful you are

Yup, it's true. When I shaved off all my hair and looked in the mirror, I saw the real me for the very first time, and the person I saw was more beautiful than the one I ever saw with hair.

Fun fact - when I started telling folks my hair is gone, they all began offering me wigs and stylish hats. Even when I say I'm fine, I like the new bald me, they kind of insisted I try them. Remember, someone's desire to put a hat or wig on you is about them, not about you. **You do you any way you want to, and have the time of your life doing it!**

Chapter 6 - A Cat and a Mat

Jill is my cat. She is also my yoga buddy. When I get up in the morning, she is usually on my yoga mat, waiting. I can see her from my bed, front paws tucked under her, eyes fixed on me, a mystical yogic force in the form of an imperturbable cat.

Jill is convinced that there is a particular time of the morning that is the preferred time to practice, and if I don't show up for it, she comes looking for me. She leaps on the bed, landing in stealth mode, her arrival barely perceptible, then with ten-pound paws she makes her presence know. It is frightening how accurate such a small being can be as she wanders aimlessly around the bed, motoring along on ecstatic purrs. The innocent placement of a paw to the groin or breast followed by the full transfer of her scant ten pounds is agonizing, and effective. It signals that all efforts to coax her into curling up for some additional shut-eye will fail and it is indeed time for yoga.

She is right, of course. There is a certain time in the morning, the sweet spot between too early and the world is waking up, when there is a quietness to the day that lends itself to mental, physical, and spiritual introspection. At the crossroads where evening winds down and the morning contemplates its beginning, where the birds are just considering their first song of the day and the neighbors are still asleep, in this sweet spot there are no random thoughts swirling around, mine or anyone else's, to distract me. No one is worrying or frowning, it's just me, a cat, and a mat.

So, what is it for me that makes practicing with Jill so special? So far, reading this, she probably sounds like a royal pain in the neck. Not so. Truth be told, she always seems to know exactly what I need. I have found if I let go of my expectations for my practice and let her guide me, I am more likely to reach a Zen place through my yoga than if I try to wrangle her out of the way. She directs me with her body, which is usually planted somewhere on my mat. Sometimes she is at the end of the mat, but on those days when she thinks I really need to take it down a notch, she will be smack-dab in the middle, purring away. There was a time when I would nudge her aside, frustrated by her insistence, and I have to admit even now there are times when I am tempted. In those moments, on the cusp of irritation, I let it all go, and I follow her lead. It is in these moments of surrender that I have learned my greatest lessons.

Just breathe - When I let go of my attachment to the poses, I find my breath. When your blood cell count is seesawing from treatment to treatment, breath and air become a precious commodity, so you start to pay close attention. Really close attention. It was in these moments, as I searched for air, that I discovered that the practice had ceased to be about the poses, that it was really never about the poses. I realized that the poses are the choreography and the breath is my real dance partner. Then, and only then, was I free to really dance.

Grace - There is a certain grace to be had when you are moving around a precious object that is oblivious to your footfalls or foot placement. When the attention shifts to the space between the poses rather than the intensity of each hold, I find I move into an entirely different place in my practice. I also find that when I have embraced that place, Jill moves to the side, giving me liberty to explore my new zone, engage in my new rhythm, explore my newfound grace.

Self-love - When I practice yoga, everything superficial fades away. The compassionate hug of muscle to bone, coaxing me to stand or sit a little taller, stays with me long after the practice is over. It is this empathy for myself that gives me the strength to endure, to stand tall in the face of it. When a small voice asks, "Are you sure?" I can confidently say, "Yes, I am sure." I am sure that I matter, and that I count. And I can do this.

Companionship - I never underestimate the unconditional love and companionship that Jill provides. She's a cat; by the definition of her species she has no use for me. And yet she is devoted. She is there by the door when I come home at night. She follows me around the house and is always up for a playful round of hide-and-seek or tag, for no other reason than we are both there and the time is right. She spends quality time with me on my yoga mat, meditation cushion, and at night when I go to sleep. There is something very comforting in having a small ball of fur curled up by your side purring maniacally in ecstasy just because she is near you. In the end, when it is just me, she makes a point to be there to remind me I am not alone. And I make sure she knows she is not alone either.

Today is just one day - Every day is precious, but today is just one day. I used to be extremely routine oriented. With cancer, that pretty much goes out the window. I have let go of my checklist of items that made each day a productive day and replaced it with the wonder of the things that come my way as gifts on any given day. Spending time on my yoga mat is spending time, as I no longer have an attachment to how long. The most important parts of my day are the moments I spend with my husband, Ken, and Jill; the moments I spend on the phone speaking with my mother and Monty, my family and friends; the moments I spend with myself in meditation. These are the moments that bring me closer to the heart, that bathe my world in love.

It all starts with a cat and a mat. I suppose it could also work with a dog and a mat. In the end, it's really about love. Surround yourself with souls that love you and the world will open up in the most amazing way.

Chapter 7 - Life, It's All Around You

Life, it's all around you. And so is "stuff." It's everywhere. I'm not sure when it happened, that the human race converted from living experientially to engaging in a hectic, frenetic race of accumulation. When did bigger, better, and latest become our stimuli, rather than being fully in the moment?

It seems with our roots in hunter-gathering, we easily fall victim to the urge to accumulate. I think there are two broad camps of accumulators - those who go for "stuff" and those who deny themselves "stuff" in order to accumulate money. Me, I bought into the accumulation credo too. I have dabbled at the edges of the denial camp for most of my life, forgoing basics that I recast as frivolities, and therefore optional, in lieu of saving. Which are you? Do you wear your underwear and socks *way* past their expiration date in order to save, or do you have the latest gadget on pre-order the day the ad goes up? From where I sit now, neither is very healthy. Neither is truly living. Whenever we enslave ourselves to an external notion for our happiness or pleasure, then we stop living authentically.

For me, the saddest part is the untold experiences I could have had that I missed out on. Being so focused on the saving part of life, I stopped paying attention to the everyday wonders that were going on around me, unnoticed.

I missed the world going on around me—the parade of birds of every shape and size and color, the cacophony of sounds that come from living in an urban environment, the potpourri of smells, the plants and flowers and trees and bugs and squirrels and people.

I missed time with my family, because I was working late on a project that could just have easily been finished the next day.

I missed the peacefulness that comes from a life truly engaged in.

I was, in truth, missing it all.

I remember driving around at night in my convertible, top down, letting the smells drift by. I wasn't going anywhere in particular; I was just enjoying the sensations. I could tell when I passed an orange grove, or a lake, or a pine forest. The scents were their calling cards, announcing their entrances and exits. I don't know why I stopped doing that. I enjoyed it, yet I let it go. I was focused on accumulation. The simple pleasures had no place, so I let them fade away. They were too easy, too attainable. I was after more difficult stimuli.

I remember taking my camera everywhere with me. I liked to capture my experiences of the amazing things I saw during the normal course of the day. I don't know why I stopped doing that either. It's ironic, really, since now I have a camera with me everywhere I go, whether I think to bring it or not, but I only focus on the phone and calendar aspect of the device. Lately, I've started to look back through my old photos. There is nothing glaringly unique about the people, or the places, or the things in them, except that they are a testament to the beauty of a moment. They are an homage to life, to being present in the moment. I miss that, a lot.

Photos take me back to a time when I was engaged with my surroundings. A time when I paid more attention to what went on around me than to my calendar or my phone. Looking back through them is helping me to reevaluate and reassess my thought process, to pay more attention to what is going on around me, to what wonders I have been missing, to what matters. I'm reconnecting with what is important - the here and now.

For me, it is through photos and writing; for you, it may be through sketching or painting or sewing or cooking, or any number of pleasurable activities you used to do and gave up. Maybe it's just being present and telling someone about the experience later. The point is, take the time to take it all in. Absorb the simple things that are going on around you all the time, engage in the things that bring happiness to your life. The big things, they'll still be there tomorrow. Or who knows, maybe they'll take care of themselves.

Chapter 8 - Staying Up in the Downstream

There is a thin line that separates happy tears and sad tears. I don't know what it is or where it is, or even if it is important. In the end, I find that crying helps regardless of the impetus. It may be disconcerting to others to see you cry, but so be it. It helps. It lets off a little steam, takes the edge off, brings you back to earth. It doesn't ease the fear or erase the doubt, but sometimes I just need a little help getting back to center, and tears are it.

Over the past two months, I have really had nothing to cry about. Things roller coaster-ed along on a set track and I went along for the ride, ups and downs planned and in stride. Then I got sick. A cold I think, just a random thing, but it showed up four days after my fourth chemo session and by the next morning it was on the fast track. My sinuses seemed embroiled in competition with my lungs to see which could produce the more serious infection first— sinusitis or bronchitis, maybe pneumonia—winner take all. My fever was over the "call the oncologist"" threshold of 100.3 degrees, so I called his nurse. He sent me to my primary care physician ASAP.

It is here I have to once again point out that I have an excellent team of caregivers. Oncologist, nurses, nurse navigators, primary care physician. Get goods ones; ones that care about you, understand the emotional complexities of the situation, and who will see you on a moment's notice.

I was at my primary care physician within two hours. My fever had climbed to 101 degrees, but I was pre-infection on all fronts— lungs and sinuses—so he prescribed a preemptive Z-pack and Mucinex to keep everything draining. And then I waited.

For three days I slept, sipped orange juice, nibbled toast, and cried. I cried at night, silently in the dark. I cried in the day, alone in front of the television. I held Ken's hand and blubbered out my fears. It helped, but in some ways it frightened me more. It frightened me that I had found something to cry about.

By Thursday, I had rallied enough to put together a simple roast-chicken-and-mashed-potatoes Thanksgiving dinner for Ken and I, then I went back to bed, and cried some more.

It is a scary, scary thing, to get sick post-chemo when you know your white blood cells are dying. I found myself counting over and over again in my head the days since chemo, the days until my low blood-count point, the days since I got a cold, as though the math would magically suddenly work itself out. In the end, there is no getting around it. Getting a cold with a compromised immune system struck terror into my heart. It is an unshakable fear, likely somewhat irrational, but mine nonetheless. I have never been afraid of dying of cancer; I am afraid of succumbing to a fluke side germ that found me at the wrong time.

It is now nearly a week later and I am beginning to come out the other side. This side germ didn't win, not by a long shot. The little rascal did mess with my Thanksgiving, a time when I traditionally reflect back on the blessings in my life, which are the people, so I want to take this moment to reflect back and thank everyone who has rallied around me, each in your own way, to make me feel loved and cared about:

First on the list, my husband, Ken, who is here with me every step of the way, encouraging me to slog on, holding me, hearing me, loving me. He is my rock, my angel, my love.

My mother, and of course, Monty, who call me every day just to check in (three times a day while I have been sick), to let me know that they are out there, caring, worrying, loving me.

My mother-in-law, Connie, who sends me cards to let me know that she is thinking about me, praying for me, loving me.

Jill, my yoga buddy, snuggle partner, and all-around cat extraordinaire, who always seems to know when I could use a soft coat to absently stroke, a warm body to snuggle close, the healing vibration of her purr to soothe me.

Danny and Jo, who talk with me and laugh with me and encourage me.

Brent and Trudy, who email and text me when I least expect it, connecting me to lifelines I didn't even know I had.

Friends and family who call, write, pray, laugh and hope. And those who share stories of their own breast cancer adventures, of coming out the other side, of moving on.

And all of you who read my blog and now are reading my book, who care enough to spend time with my thoughts and follow my adventure. Happy Thanks-for-Giving!

Chapter 9 - The Changing Landscape of My Tongue

Taste. We take it for granted. We know what we like, and what we don't. We sample things within our spectrum of acceptance, leaving the suspect items for someone else to try. These tried-and-true rules of engagement give us comfort. We don't question our likes and dislikes, they just are. And then they aren't.

I was warned that my sense of taste would change. The chemo kills the fast-growing cells in your body, including your taste buds, so as they die off and regroup, the landscape of your mouth changes. Only, it's not just your sense of taste, it's also the consistency of things. I was prepared to suddenly find something I liked tasted off, but when something I like still tastes the same—good—yet the consistency is unbearable, that's just not fair.

The first thing to go was cashews. They taste fine, but they have a mealy consistency that is stomach churning. Next came bananas. They don't taste bad and the consistency is fine, but when I eat them, my taste center gets confused. It can't decide if they are okay or not, and it short circuits into anxiety. Then, just when I was getting the hang of this random deletion of foods from my repertoire, I started to crave things I hadn't eaten in years and didn't really like. So what's a gal to do, but go with it. I eat what works, skip what doesn't, listen to my body and see what it calls for next.

So far ...

- For the first five weeks after my first chemo treatment, I craved kiwi fruit. I ate two a night, every night, as a snack. I couldn't get enough of them. Then the desire died out as suddenly as it arose.

- Watermelon - I love watermelon. It's the perfect food - cool, refreshing, watery, and full of electrolytes. I used to eat watermelon every day until I started chemo. Then all of a sudden it didn't sound that appetizing. It didn't taste bad and the consistency was fine, it just didn't sound like it would sit right in my stomach. Now, eight weeks in, it is starting to sound good again. Go figure.

- Berries - I love raspberries and blueberries, but whenever I eat them, I get a latent moldy taste in my mouth. I can't believe that every berry I buy is moldy, so I'm giving up until after chemo. I don't want to ruin my chances of ever eating berries again.

- Cashews - They taste fine, but the consistency gives you a flash that you are chewing on a mouthful of maggots. Not good.

- Chicken - I used to be a thigh person, but lately I have been craving breast meat. I don't know why. White meat is dry and chewy, but in my brain it is the better choice, even though it doesn't taste that way.

-Steak - I hadn't eaten steak in years, then all of a sudden it sounded good again. I made filet mignon tacos and pizza a couple of times and then the desire died out as quickly as it came. Sometimes I eat steak and it tastes good, other days like dried blood. I think that chapter is closed.

- Cinnamon Raisin Bread - All of a sudden this has become my go-to breakfast and snack food, although I never ate it before chemo. I make it homemade in the bread-maker with all-organic ingredients. It calms my stomach in the morning and even makes for a great evening snack. Hmmm ... I hear a piece with my name on it calling to me as I write ...

- Canary melons - Never mind that they taste insanely good, but there is something in their chemical makeup that soothes my stomach, and my brain knows it!

- Pizza - I'm not a big pizza eater, but lately it has a delightful ring to it. Pre-chemo, it was too doughy and didn't sit well. Now, I'm all about Amy's Organic Margherita Pizza. I put broccoli on top and it makes for a delightful easy meal.

So there you have it. It's not that the food choices are so strange, it's just that they haven't really been mine. It's okay though, whatever works, for now. It's not forever, it's just for now. When all this is over, I can move on to whatever my new normal will be. Who knows, some of these food choices may even stick around and be part of that. I'm voting for the cinnamon raisin bread.

Chapter 10 - Blessed Are We

I am blessed. When I think of all the things that can happen to a person in their lifetime, I look at the vast spectrum and know I am truly blessed. Do you know that I have gone my entire life and the only bone I have ever broken is my big toe? Freak accident, really. I was horseback riding, standing in the center of the ring while another rider jumped the course, when another waiting horse got belligerent and kicked out at Jon Tu, my horse. He likely had it coming, he could be a brat at times. I didn't think anything of it at the time, but woke up the next morning in excruciating pain, barely able to walk. A trip to the doctor confirmed it—a broken big toe. I was on crutches for weeks. The strange thing was, I rode my bike home from the barn the night before, after it was broken, and didn't feel a thing. That's it for broken bones, though, my left big toe.

I've had stitches once in my life too. Another funny story. I was young, probably around twenty, headed off to my first day of work at my new job. I wanted to see the full length of my outfit in the mirror before I left, because that's what you do when you're twenty (and thirty, and forty, and fifty ...) so I got the bright idea to stand on a table to use the long mirror over the hall desk. The only table in there was a small, round, ceramic table, more of an end table really, or a plant stand. I'm sure you can figure out how that ended. Not well. Suffice it to say, a ceramic table will not hold the weight of an adult. Dozens of stitches later, my calf was put back together, but I did miss my first day of work.

These are minor faux pas, though. I have never been injured in a car accident, or a bike accident, or a riding accident. I've never been hit by a car, or a person. I've never been seriously bitten by a dog, or a cat, or any other animal for that matter.

When I go to the doctor, I check "no" to everything on that list of common issues. You know the list - diabetes, heart disease, arthritis, Crohn's Disease, ulcers, indigestion, eye problems, ear problems, gut problems, migraines, in general any of the something-is-making-me-miserable problems. Oh, and here's a big one, I'm not in pain. Nothing chronic in my repertoire. I'm truly blessed.

I have a great job that I love; I work with people that I care deeply about, and who seem to care deeply about me.

I have a loving, caring family that I talk to regularly. Sure, we have our moments, but I wouldn't trade a one of them.

I talk to my mother every day. I catch up on her world and fill her in on mine. These conversations are priceless and they are the highlight of my morning, each and every day. It's not that we talk about anything that important or earth shattering, it's just that I get to hear her voice, to hear that she is happy. When I know that, all is right in the world, all is right in my world.

I have a wonderful, loving husband, Ken. He is my angel, my rock, my north star. He keeps me focused on what is important in life - love. That's it. Loving one another deeply, unconditionally, and with complete acceptance and support. He exemplifies that love each and every day in the little things he does, and the big way he is present in our marriage. He takes me to all my chemo sessions, sits with me, is there for me. Just having him there is a calming influence for me. I know he has my back, will make sure nothing goes awry. With the Taxol treatment, they give you Benadryl beforehand to mitigate any reaction to it and it puts me to sleep. That's a tricky thing when I'm supposed to keep my hands and feet on ice packs the whole time. He makes sure my hands and feet do what they are supposed to while I'm drifting in and out. He also wakes me up when they bring around the warm cookies and feeds me an oatmeal raisin cookie (since I don't have a free hand). He's an angel, my twin flame, the love of my life, in this life and all lives.

So really, I'm blessed. The breast cancer thing, it's just a thing. I'm blessed there too. It's just breast cancer. It's in one spot, it's treatable, and it's shrinking. I have a great team of doctors at UF Health Breast Cancer Center in Orlando helping me with this -

Dr. Regan Rostorfer is my oncologist, and a more knowledgeable, educated, caring, approachable, and genuinely delightful person you will not find. I lob a lot of questions his way, some crazy some not, and he walks me through all my concerns and ideas with patience and joy. And if I don't get it all the first time, he walks me through it again. He's a traditional medical doctor, but he listens to my holistic ideas and navigates them with ease and understanding. While his treatments are traditional, he doesn't discount any of the natural remedies I come up with as long as we discuss them together and he knows one won't interfere with the other. Makes perfect sense to me.

Dr. Jeffrey R. Smith is my surgeon. He too has infinite patience with my endless supply of questions. He put my port in and it was a fabulous experience. It is that surgery experience at the UF Health Ambulatory Surgery Center that prompted the nickname "the Orlando Health Spa." I won't see Dr. Smith again until my chemo comes to an end and it is time to talk about surgery. When that time comes, I know it will be an open, honest dialogue about what is in my best interests, and the decision will ultimately be mine. My decision will be based on knowing all the options and the recurrence statistics that come with those options as well as any post-surgery treatments that are recommended with the different surgery options. Lots of options, lots of right answers. In the end, the navigation will be about what is best for me personally, and Dr. Smith is not only a great surgeon, but he is a great listener and explainer.

Laura Martin, RN, MS, CBCN - Laura is my nurse navigator, a central clearing house of sorts for questions and concerns that have to do with everyone and everything involved in my treatment. Laura has been a godsend. She is always available to discuss any and all concerns and questions I may have and can navigate any problem with ease. When all my tests were done and it was time to start my chemo, the first date they could give me was three weeks out. After wading through three months of testing and knowing what my diagnosis was, I was ready to get the ball rolling. I called Laura and the appointment was moved up to the end of that week. Laura listens, cares, and gets things done. She is, in short, an angel.

Nurses, nurses, nurses - a shout-out to all the nurses at UF Health Breast Cancer Center. Dr. Rostorfer's and Dr. Smith's nurses, who are always available to talk and answer questions, the draw-station and chemo nurses on the chemo floor who are always friendly and caring. As an aside, when you have a good nurse and you have a good experience, tell them so! I always thank the nurses for what they do. Yesterday I had Joy as my chemo nurse. She was delightful in every way. And I had a male draw-station nurse, my first! He works in the ER and then works as a draw-station nurse as well. He finds it to be a nice balance between crazy and calm. He was dynamite, and I told him so!

The thing with breast cancer is that it's not really a one-and-done situation with any of your doctors (or nurses). There are endless meetings and options to go over, and then if anything changes you get to go over it all again. This process has definitely taught me to slow down, take a step back, and live in the present. When I was first diagnosed, I wanted to just get it all done and over with, to have surgery and move on with my life. It's never that simple. Surgery is now months away and I don't think about it. There really isn't anything to think about, because I'm not close enough to know my options. Right now I'm focused on chemotherapy, Taxol to be specific, and mitigating neuropathy.

It's a good thing, though, this slowing down. Meditation is helping with it too. I meditate fifteen to thirty minutes every morning, clear my head, and focus on the brightness in the world. I welcome peace and joy into my life and sweep out stress, frustration, and anger. I am thankful for all the blessings in my life, and try to remember that the other stuff is just a gateway to appreciate those blessings even more. In the end, there is nothing good or bad in life, there are just things that we attach meaning to. We can change that internal dialogue, those labels, whenever we want to. I'm changing mine. I am blessed, truly blessed.

Now it's your turn ...

Chapter 11 - A Christmas Miracle

I believe in miracles. They happen all the time. We don't often pay attention to them, and even more often we take them for granted, but they happen, nonetheless. With cancer, I spend a lot of time being grateful, acknowledging the miracles big and small happening in my life day in and day out. I am extremely grateful for the resilience of my body, that I wake up every day feeling really pretty darn good and can lead a relatively normal life during my treatment. I am grateful for the people in my life - my husband, Ken; my family; my cat, Jill; my co-workers; my friends; my doctors. And I am grateful that my cancer is localized, that it is treatable, that it is responding to treatment. I thank anyone and everyone in the miracle department, whoever and whatever they may be, for all the blessings in my life as often as I can. I read the news, I know how much worse it could be, and I am forever grateful that it is not.

That is not my Christmas miracle, though. Sometimes, when things happen to us, they are really meant to inspire someone else, show them that there is good in the world, that if you believe, that if you ask, good things will come your way. I didn't realize it at the time, but now that it is all done and over with, this particular miracle was also for Ken. Here is the story ...

On the evening of Friday, December 9, 2016, I lost my wedding ring. I was sitting on the couch with Ken. He had just gotten home from work and was eating a sandwich. We were spending a few precious moments together before I headed off to bed. With the cancer, I try to get to bed before 10 p.m. so I have enough time to get up several times in the night to drink water and pee and still get in at least seven hours of sleep. I reached for my ring to center it on the top of my ring finger like I do periodically throughout the day, every day, and it wasn't there. I rifled through the blanket I was snuggled in, hoping against all hope that it had just fallen off and was right there with me, but it wasn't. It was gone. In that one instant, I also realized I had no idea when or where I had lost it.

Did I lose it at work? At the grocery store on the way home? Did it go down the sink when I did dishes? Was it in the garbage? Tangled up in a piece of clothing somewhere? And with chemo brain, I honestly couldn't say when was the last time I saw it, or felt it. It was all a muddle, the recent past no more distinct than the distant.

We scrambled around for a bit, or really Ken did, trying to find it. He searched my car, went through the garbage, looked down the garbage disposal. I asked him to stop. It broke my heart to find him crouched on the floor going through the garbage piece by piece. I shuffled off to the bedroom, brushed my teeth, curled up in bed, and cried. It was gone. The ring we had designed together, the identical mate to the one that Ken wears on his hand, the ring that before God and family he had put on my hand to bind our lives together, "forever and always, and then some." It was gone. When he came in to check on me, we cried together.

It's powerful, the emotion that one tiny ring holds.

The day after I lost it, I did what I always do these days when something is bothering me - I meditated on it. I find that when I sit with my thoughts, really sit, and let the universe in, the answers come. In this instance, the message came loud and clear, "let it go." So I did. I won't say it was easy, but I let it all go, the tears, the sadness, the attachment (that part was really hard!). As much as that ring meant to me, to us, what it stands for is still alive and strong, and that is what is really important.

The best thing to do when letting something go is to really let it go, and distract yourself, so Ken and I decided to head to Mt. Dora to Long & Scott's Corn Maze. It was the last weekend of the maze and we had never been, so I figured why not. A day out in the sunshine and fresh air, walking through a corn maze, it sounded like the ideal distraction. The maze is set up as a game field of sorts. You get a game card and wander through the maze looking for game stations and collecting clues to fill out your card. It was a beautiful day, not too hot and not too cold. Ken and I spent a wonderful afternoon out in the air, I got some great photos of ears of corn, and we learned some fun facts about the State of Florida. For instance, the state flower is the orange blossom, the state bird is the mockingbird, and the state song is "The Swanee River." You get the point. Then we went home, had a nice dinner, watched Christmas movies, and went to bed. Sure, we talked about it, but we had what was important, each other. If the ring was meant to come back, it would find its way back to me. I had let it go.

On Sunday, we cuddled in, using the morning to just enjoy being together without having to be anywhere or go anywhere. Later, we headed off to get in some Christmas shopping. On the way home, we stopped at Publix to pick up dinner, and Ken said we should go to the Customer Service desk and ask if someone had turned in a ring. I agreed. I had planned to do the same next time I was here.

Ken showed the gal at the Customer Service desk his ring, telling her "it looks just like this one." The rings are white gold with two yellow gold people, arms stretched toward one another, holding either side of a rose gold heart. They form an infinity sign, representing how long we will love one another, "always and forever, and then some." The gal went to check while we waited.

And waited.

I had mixed feelings on getting my hopes up. My fingers are tiny. The ring takes up the footprint of about a dime. The chances that someone could see it on the floor were a long shot.

Our wait stretched on.

She seemed to be looking for something, and after lots of rummaging around and inquiring on her part, she reappeared and held out my ring.

My wedding ring, my precious, precious wedding ring! I couldn't believe it!

She said someone had found it and turned it in the day before. I was stunned. I started crying, Ken started crying. I hugged the girl at least three times. I couldn't believe it, my ring had come back to me!

I don't know who turned my ring in. I don't know where they found it, or what circumstances led them to turn it in. All I know is, I'm grateful, so very, very grateful. I'm grateful for the power of prayer, meditation, and whispers. I'm grateful for angels who hear those prayers, meditations, and whispers and pass them on, prompting chain reactions of events we can only guess at. I am grateful for those with open hearts that hear the whispers of angels, who act as instruments for good, who answer prayers they have no knowledge of. Whoever you are, wherever you are, thank you, thank you, thank you! Thank you for this Christmas miracle.

It wasn't until a few days later than my husband, Ken, shared with me how meaningful finding my ring had been. Miracles touch a place in us that we don't think is reachable. In this case, finding the ring had restored some faith in mankind in him, began to heal a part of his soul that gets chipped away at each day by the horrors reported on the news, the unkindness drivers lavish on one another on the road, the disregard neighbors have for one another, living as though no one can see or hear what goes on beyond their property line. It reminded him that we invite into our lives what we focus on, so if we believe in and look for the good in people, we will find it, and eventually it will even outweigh the petty injustices that we believe used to prevail.

For all of you out there who do the right thing, each and every day, in your own unique way you do the work of angels, and the world is a better place for it. Thank you!

Chapter 12 - I Believe in Santa Claus

This year, Ken and I are staying home for Christmas. With chemo once a week, the driving seemed like too much, so for the first time EVER, we have put up a real honest-to-goodness Christmas tree. Not a mini tree, not a tabletop tree, a seven-and-a-half-foot tree with lights and ornaments and the whole shebang. (Thanks to Balsam Hill, no living trees were harmed to accomplish this undertaking.) We have never bothered with a tree in the past since we were always somewhere else for Christmas, but not this year. This year, I am setting the stage. This year, Santa Claus is coming, to my house!

First thing on my to-do list for this stay-at-home Christmas year was to rev up the Christmas spirit. The tree went up in the beginning of November. We put it up when it arrived. No time like the present, and with chemo, no guarantees on energy level in the future. I do things when the mood strikes me, which, in this instance, was in the glow of tree-arrival excitement. We light it every night, in addition to our small tabletop poinsettia tree.

I've also been watching Christmas movies. I started with the Hallmark Channel, which I indulge in every year, but after a few weeks of that they were into reruns, so I moved on to our personal collection. We have several favorites that we try and watch every year: *Christmas in Connecticut,* (with Barbara Stanwyck), *The Holiday* (Kate Winslett, Cameron Diaz, Jack Black, and Jude Law), *A Christmas Story, Peanut's Christmas, The Ref* (Denis Leary and Kevin Spacey), *Love Actually*, and of course some of the BHC movies - Beloved Holiday Classics - *Rudolph the Red-Nosed Reindeer, Frosty the Snowman, Santa Claus is Comin' to Town* (nothing says Christmas like the Burgermeister Meisterburger, Heat Miser and Cold Miser), and of course, *The Polar Express.* This year we even found an old Dickens story about a cricket on a hearth, aptly named *The Cricket on the Hearth.* Not sure on the meaning in the story, but apparently it's good luck in England to have a cricket camped out on your hearth. I am quite fond of the older Christmas stories, as you can see. They have a simplicity to them that I am drawn to.

Next on my tour of spirit-inducing experiences was the theater. This year, the Orlando Shakespeare Theater was doing my favorite holiday play, *Every Christmas Story Ever Told (And Then Some)*, so I put my phobia for the germy public aside and went. For those thinking I was taking my life in my hands just to see a play, it's really not as bad as all that. The show was in the theater in the round performance space, which has lots of places I could sit with no one around me if it came to that, but we had seats around seemingly healthy folks and my white blood count has been pretty steady, so I was comfortable. Nary a cough or sneeze was heard the entire time.

Anyway, back to the play. The show is a hysterical three-man romp that begins as the telling of *A Christmas Carol* and turns into a whirlwind telling and/or reference to all the beloved Christmas classics with sidebars of Christmas traditions around the world sprinkled in and finishing with a side-splitting round of all the beloved Christmas carols ever sung. I have seen this show at least three times. I go every time the Orlando Shakespeare Theater puts it on. They do change it up a little each time they stage it, but even if they didn't, I would go. It is just plain funny. It's irreverent, sassy, and vaudeville-ish, but it's also a great way to really bring home the meaning of Christmas. It is here, at this show, that I found the answer that I was looking for, oddly enough. You see, Christmas spirit is many things to many people, but believing in the spirit of Santa Claus, that is the key to it all.

So here is where this takes a turn. In the end, this isn't really about Christmas or Santa, it's about the magic of letting go, of letting yourself step into the realm of the impossible and entertaining the belief that maybe, just maybe, it could be. When we are children, we are told the story of the man with the red suit coming in his sleigh pulled by reindeer. We are taught to, encouraged to, believe in Santa Claus. I see it as part of our creative growth, like playing with dolls and trucks, or recreating your favorite television show or movie in the backyard or basement. It's make-believe, yes, but it is also creativity in its purest form, and an important part of development. We imagine the impossible, learning critical skills so that when we grow up, we can make the impossible come true, each and every day, in our work and hopefully still in our leisure. Everything we do in life has the magical touch of creativity to it. Whether we are doctors saving lives, architects designing homes, construction workers putting a home together or fixing a damaged one, office workers creating processes to improve productivity or customer relations, it all hinges on creativity and our ability to think beyond what we know, to believe in what is not yet possible.

Why then, is no longer believing in Santa, the Easter bunny, the tooth fairy, or any of our childhood belief systems, a rite of passage to adulthood? Why not keep them, like old friends, and continue to feed off the creative energy they provide? They are no different than any other fable or tale we tell our children, or ourselves, so why put so much effort into denying or affirming their existence? We don't spend that kind of time considering the likelihood that Mother Goose actually lived in a shoe with all those children. No one goes over the Grimm Fairy Tales with a fine-tooth comb and wonders how it was possible that a witch lived in the woods eating children all her life and no one noticed they were missing. We know they are just tales, creative imaginings to encourage a behavior or teach lessons, but also to light a candle in the deepest recess of our being that calls, "just maybe ..." And so are our holiday stories of Santa and Frosty and Jack Frost and the Easter Bunny. Without them, we become stale, our magical well begins to dry up.

I like the movie *The Polar Express.* It gets me the closest to what I am trying to say. The part at the end where the boy shakes the bell from Santa's sleigh and can't hear its ring, then decides to believe and he can hear it, that is the beginning of the journey right there. You have to decide to believe. (No nitpicking that he saw Santa so seeing is believing.)

Now this is a special kind of believing. I'm not saying that I believe Santa Claus is actually coming on Christmas for real, or that the tooth fairy will come without help from mom or dad, this is about opening yourself up to the magical power of make-believe, of letting your imagination fuel your creativity unfettered and without judgment. Of taking in these stories, and all fables and tall tales, and letting the magic of the space they create take hold and fuel your own creative genius. These creative ideas hold a magical power all their own, so if we believe in them, let them do their work, then good things happen. To this end, I also believe in fairies, gnomes, trolls, angels, ghosts (only nice ones), the list is likely endless, like my imagination. When you open yourself up to everything, anything is possible ...

So this year, Santa Claus in all his splendor is coming to my house, through a Christmas tree, holiday movies and theater, and holiday songs. It's not too late, let the magic ensue at your house! Oh, and feel free to substitute Santa Claus and Christmas with any beloved winter holiday figures and tales of your choosing. This isn't about religion, though, this is about magic, so pick the ones that are make-believe!

Chapter 13 - The Trouble with Taxol

I am now in phase two of my chemo regimen, the Taxol phase. Twelve weeks of Taxol, once per week. Every Thursday, to be exact. I have to say, I entered this phase with much angst and trepidation, but as is the case with most worry, it was time wasted. For one thing, the side effects are much less than in phase one, and there isn't the dreaded Neulasta shot the day afterwards. That's not to say it still isn't poison, it just seems to be a more palatable version.

The one downside and potential side effect, which is what caused all the angst, is that Taxol can cause neuropathy, or damage to the peripheral nerves, mainly the nerve endings in the hands and feet. To combat this, while I have the treatment I have my hands and feet parked on frozen peas. I start fifteen minutes before the treatment, keep them on the entire treatment, and wait until fifteen minutes after to remove them. The theory behind it is that if you keep your hands and feet cold, the blood vessels will shrink and you won't get as much of the drug in that area.

Technically, you are supposed to do like fifteen minutes on and fifteen minutes off, but the pre-chemo medication they give me, specifically Benadryl, puts me to sleep, so I have set up a system where I put my hands and feet in socks, bend my knees so my feet can be flat on the peas, wedge pillows between my knees and the arms of the chair so when I fall asleep nothing flops over, and then put my hands on the arms of the chair with frozen peas under the palms. This way I can nod off without messing up the setup. Ken wakes me up when it's over. It seems to be working so far.

The one mishap, or really scare, I had was the first week. The treatment went fine, but I didn't seem to get, or don't recall getting, the memo that you shouldn't put your hands in hot water, or even warm water, after receiving Taxol infusions. The day after the treatment I felt fine and went on my merry way, doing dishes, taking a hot shower, washing my hands in warm water. I mean, it's technically winter here in Florida, so why would I use cold water for anything? The palms of my hands felt a little warm during the day, but I didn't think anything of it, because some tingling the next day is normal. They said it would go away. Well, I woke up Saturday morning with my fingertips bright red and puffy and all tactile sense gone. I could tell I was touching something, but I couldn't feel the texture. It was pretty scary, being that I had eleven more treatments to go. So I did the dutiful patient thing and called the nurse on Monday and explained my symptoms. She got hold of the doctor and his verdict was try it one more time and see if it happens again. Meanwhile, the nurse told me that I could use cold water or ice packs after the treatment if I felt any symptoms coming on, so I started doing everything with my hands in cool water and after a day or so my hands went back to normal.

Well, for round two of the Taxol, I didn't take any chances. My life is now lukewarm showers and washing my hands in tepid water. I usually finish off with a douse of cold water for good measure. So far, so good. I have gone through four treatments with no recurrence of what happened the first time. I have chalked it up to "my bad" and moved on. The nurses ask me about it every time, how are my hands, did it reoccur, and I admit "my bad" every time. You have to own your stuff in this world, and that one was 100% mine!

Several things gnawed at me during the whole episode, but the main one was that my hands reacted so badly and my feet were fine. Also, it came on fast and furious when it should have been gradual. If I was truly reacting that badly to the drug, it should have been my hands and feet, not just my hands. It just didn't make sense to me. The Internet can be a dangerous thing when you have cancer and are being infused with poison, so tread lightly, my friends, but I braved it and found enough solid information from reputable sights to find out that I was probably okay and as long as I stayed away from the hot water, it wouldn't recur.

So that's the trouble with Taxol. All in all, though, it is a much easier course than the first-phase drugs were. I am sleepy the day of treatment from the pre-meds, but then up at 4:30 a.m. the next morning, raring to go. I'm full of energy, have no nausea, achiness, flu symptoms (Neulasta—blech!), no shortness of breath, no nothing. I generally run out of gas around 9 or 9:30 p.m., but heck, I got up before the birds, so I'm going to give myself that one.

I'm a happy camper, all in all. My spirits are good, I am confident in the angels watching over me and guiding me through this adventure, in Dr. Rostorfer's skills, in the power of the prayers that are said for me each day (keep them coming!) and in the power of meditation and yoga and the healing effects they have. Healing is a multi-faceted process, so I'm giving all the layers—mind, body and spirit—equal attention and love.

Chapter 14 - The Panacea of a Cat's Purr

There is something about a cat's purr. No one really knows why they purr, or what it does, but for me, the purr of my cat, my friend, my ally, is a panacea that heals all ills. Jill is a Humane Society rescue and was a tough one to win over despite being adopted as a kitten, but over time she and I have formed a special bond. Now she sleeps with me at night, lulling me to sleep with her purr while I stroke her hair. I have always found it fascinating that when a cat is happy their hair gets softer. Jill has hair like an angora rabbit.

With cancer, I find I spend a lot more time living in the moment. The here and now is where our experiences happen, so to really live life, that is the best place to park yourself. Pre-cancer, I did what most people do, I went through the motions of now with my head in the future, planning what was to come, only to find that when that sought-after moment came, I was missing it as well, my thoughts firmly planted on some appointment or task that was coming yet later still. Funny thing about tomorrow, it comes whether you think about it or not. You can wrangle over the details, try to get the timing of it perfect, but in the end it comes on its own and unfolds as it will. Now, I live in the moment, blissfully enthralled in what is going on right now. Yes, on occasion I feel myself slipping into old habits, drifting off into the past or future, but I coax myself back. The here and now is where the action is. The here and now is where memories are made.

One would think that with cancer and chemo, the here and now would not be such a great place to be. Not so. UF Health Cancer Center is a hive of wonderful people. Each week I get to meet a new and interesting chemo nurse, hear his/her story, find out why he or she does what they do. There is a purr about the place that always puts me at ease. Once a week I sit in a recliner (with a heater and massage function if I am so inclined), interact with really nice people, take a Benadryl-induced nap, then after a couple of hours I go home none the worse for wear.

Then there are the cookies to look forward to. They bring around warm cookies—your choice of chocolate chip, oatmeal raisin, or peanut butter. I've mentioned them before, but they really are good. Warm and soft, they melt in your mouth. If you are hungrier than that, they will gladly bring you a sandwich or a drink. The nurses and volunteers go above and beyond to ensure you are comfortable, from the warm blankets to the warm cookies, the pillows to the snacks.

I do wonder sometimes if I am slightly nuts since I kind of look forward to chemo day. It is very relaxing and, aside from the Benadryl haze, I have no side effects that I can feel. Plus, I get to spend the day with my husband, Ken. What's not to like? I'm sure there are all sorts of not-so-great things happening internally that will surface at some point, but the chemo is shrinking the tumor, aka causing the cancer to die, so there is that too. All and all, I'm embracing the moment, the good and the potentially ugly, for all it's worth.

Meditation has been key to keeping my mind in sync with the events unfolding around me. I meditate fifteen to thirty minutes every morning after yoga. I have taken a couple of meditation workshops and trainings, and the big take-aways for me were:

1 - **Be comfortable**. If you are not comfortable, you will spend a good deal of your meditation time thinking about that, so do what works for you. I sit cross-legged on the floor. You may prefer sitting on a chair or in a position with your back supported. Do what works for you.

2 - **There is no such thing as thinking of nothing.** The mind thinks, always. It is what it is designed to do, so trying to think of nothing is a losing proposition. You can, however, loosen your attachment to your thoughts, acknowledging them from afar rather than getting sucked into any drama you may have attached to them. For me, I sit with what comes up for me, letting the thoughts flow in, acknowledging them and then moving on. I invite positive thoughts in, such as peace and joy, and release negative thoughts,

such as anger, frustration, or self-doubt. If you are wondering what you need to release, just sit with your thoughts for a few minutes and let the smoke rise. Those are the emotions you need to let go of.

3- **No judgment.** Meditation is a place of peace. Don't judge your meditation, just enjoy it. Release expectations and just sit with yourself, listen to yourself, hear yourself. Your thoughts are your guide to what you need to work on.

Currently, my meditation is a hybrid of prayer and meditation. The Archangel Gabriel is my guide on this cancer adventure, so he is always with me in my meditations, as is my father, Richard. I invite any and all angels, ancestors, and ascended masters who want to join in into my meditation space. Personal growth is not an easy thing, and for once in my life I am open to listening to what the experts have to say. There is enormous comfort in knowing I am not alone, that I have support from all layers.

I have also started working with crystals. I find that when I work with crystals in my meditation, I can hear better, sort of like putting tin foil on a television antenna. I want to be sure that I understand what is being said. You'd be surprised how much our friends on the other side have to say if we just take the time to ask.

And then, of course, there is the panacea of a cat's purr. Jill sits with me while I meditate. She curls up next to my right thigh and motors on, her purr a constant reminder of the peacefulness that comes with living in, being in, engaging in, this moment, right now.

Chapter 15 - Happy Anniversary

Today is my wedding anniversary. Nine years ago today, I stood before my family and pledged my heart and soul to Ken Johnson, my best friend in the world, my lover, my twin flame. No, we don't finish each other's sentences, like all the same foods, or share all the same interests, but we complete each other's lives in a way that allows us both to grow and thrive emotionally, spiritually, and physically. We challenge each other to be better friends and neighbors; we encourage each other to reach for the stars.

We have all heard of soul mates, but a twin flame is a special kind of love. We can have many soul mates in our lives, but we only have one twin flame, someone we search for throughout all eternity, life after life, and strive to connect with over and over again. It is this one soul that completes us, perfects us, makes everything all right no matter what we are up against. For me, that soul is Ken. I have known him throughout time and am blessed to have found him again in this lifetime. The moment my eyes met his, I knew he was the one, and my search was over.

When I look around our home, and even in my closet, my favorite things are the gifts Ken has given me over the years. They are the things he picked out that he knew I would like, simple things I didn't know would be priceless to me until he wrapped them in a smile and presented them to me in a gesture of love. They are commonplace things, but they mean the world to me. They tell me he knows me in a way that matters deeply. He understands my soul.

In honor of our anniversary, here is my love letter to my husband, Ken, the man who loves me unconditionally, challenges me to chase my dreams, and will stand up to me, going toe-to-toe, which is no easy feat.

To my beloved husband, Ken, on our ninth anniversary -

I could have bought a fancy card full of mushy prose,

One that went on and on about how much I love you and how perfect we are for each other,

One that praised your good looks, your great personality, your charisma and charm,

But I decided that I would rather it come from me, from my heart, from my soul.

So here you have it, a humble piece of paper, no adornment or fluff, with my heart laid bare.

I love you to the moon and back, every day, in every way.

When I am with you, my hand in yours, I feel whole, complete, at home in the world.

When I am with you, I am at peace with myself, at home in my skin, open to what may be.

When I am with you, I am alive with creative energy, with the wonder of possibility, with the beauty that is all around me and is yet to be.

When I am with you, I can't help but smile. Your eyes are dazzling, alive with mischief lurking in the calm. Your smile melts me, and whatever seemed of concern is soon lost in the rumble of your laugh. Your scent is an aphrodisiac that draws me in, cuddles me close, tells me all is right in the world, and always will be, as long as we are together.

You are my forever love, for now and all eternity. You are my twin flame.

Our path has not always been easy, but it has always been worth it. Ours is not a giddy love, but a love that stands the test of time. It is a love that joins us together and will continue to bind us long after this lifetime has passed and is forgotten. When I look into your eyes, the soul looking back at me is ageless, timeless. I know I will always find you and you will always find me, time and time again, because we belong together.

I love you to the moon and back, and always will. I love you, with all my heart and soul.

I love you, always and forever, and then some ...

The greatest gift we have is to give of ourselves. Be open, be loud, be bold, and tell the people you love that you love them, often and without hesitation.

Chapter 16 - Time to Put on High-Topped Sneakers

The weeks are drifting by. My doctor said the twelve weeks of weekly Taxol treatments would go by quickly, and now here I am just past the halfway point. Seven down, five to go; they are marching by, hustling me forward toward an inevitable end date to my chemo and the need for me to focus on something new, like surgery.

Ah yes, a date with my surgeon, at which point the landscape of my physical being will likely be forever changed. It is something I have to think about, have to assess my next step on, but which I am continually pushing off, bargaining for time on, pretending for just one more lazy, hazy, blissful Taxol moment may not have to be.

Funny, the games we play with ourselves. Up until now, I have taken this adventure in stride, doing the legwork, making educated choices, moving toward an end goal, but now I am just a little muddled. Maybe it's the Taxol, the week-after-week of pre-chemo cocktails knocking me into a stupor, drifting off to sleep with my hands and feet on frozen pea mattresses, waking up starving with a ferocious hunger for foods that up until now have not tempted my palate.

Then there are the sleepless nights. My body has started acclimating to the Benadryl, so sleep the day of treatment has become fitful at best. I'm good for four hours the night of treatment before I wake up, usually in the middle of the night, with the zeal of the Energizer Bunny. As of late, chamomile tea has become my drug of choice, providing a partial reprieve of several hours of sleep before I am greeted by the glow of 2 a.m. on the clock face. If it wasn't so darn cold, I would get up and try to be productive, but snuggled between Ken, my husband, and Jill, our cat, in the warm cocoon of our bed is a delightful place to be no matter what time of day or night, so I watch the clock, and watch my thoughts, tick, tick, ticking along.

Watching your thoughts can be an interesting exercise, until the tables turn and you find your thoughts are watching you. There is just so much thinking you can do without your own input, which tells me I'm not really watching my thoughts, I'm just trying not to think them. And for good reason. Yes, with every treatment, I march ever closer to the end date. February sixteenth is my final chemo treatment. On that bittersweet day, I will be obliged to turn forever forward, to look toward what inevitably will be a cataclysmic shift in the physical landscape of my being.

Okay, so maybe this sounds a little dramatic, even for me, but the reality of it all is that within the next six weeks I need to dig down deep inside myself and decide whether I have the stuff it takes to pull this off, to possibly spend the latter portion of my life with one breast and be okay with it, to look myself in the mirror day after day and see myself as whole, complete, undamaged. Up until now, the physical changes that come with chemo and cancer have not really bothered me. They are, after all, temporary. Surgery is permanent. There is no going back. The landscape will be forever changed.

I do realize that all this worrying and machination is not necessary, that I have five weeks of treatment left and won't have concrete options laid out until I am done. I do realize that I am breaking my own cardinal rule, to not think about the next step until the step has to be taken, but this is gnawing at me. For some reason, this one thing is the thing, my Achilles heel of this adventure.

To bring some clarity to these machinations, I am 99% sure reconstructive surgery is not for me. From what I have learned, reconstructive surgery, like most things, comes with trade-offs, in this case aesthetics for a possible decline in functionality. Anyone who knows me knows that is not a trade I would be inclined to make. Reconstruction after a mastectomy using an implant involves separating the pectoral muscles from the rib cage so the implant can be placed under the muscle. As you will have a foreign object in your body, the reconstruction site can have its own host of problems. Then there are the follow-up requirements - MRIs every couple of years to ensure the implant is not damaged, and replacing the implant itself every ten to fifteen years (no, they don't last "forever"). All that for what I consider to be an elective aesthetic procedure. Nope, not for me. So the options then turn to lumpectomy vs. mastectomy, which also has side bars that come with them. With a lumpectomy, my doctors will 100% recommend radiation therapy, which has a long list of side effects and can do long-term damage to the lymph nodes, resulting in lymphedema. With a mastectomy, I will have one breast and may end up with a recommendation for radiation anyway. Is it any wonder my mind drifts back to this pending decision, again and again and again?

The problem with Achilles is he wore sandals, so it's time for me to put on high-topped sneakers. We are all entitled to moments of vulnerability, spaces in time when we let our guard down and pretty much say, "Holy shit, stop the train! I want to get off!" Even me. And even you. Now it's time for me to shake it off and move on.

Like I always tell my husband, Ken, there are no bad decisions, or bad choices for that matter. Our core responsibility in this gift of life we have been given is to pick the path we will travel and make decisions when we are faced with crossroads, decisions that will impact our life going forward and often the lives of those close to us. We must commit to the decisions we make and make our way, head held high, with the conviction of our choices. And if we are lucky, really lucky, we will realize the path we choose never has any bearing on whether we will reach our destination.

Life *physically* begins and moves toward a *physical* ending, it is the middle that is the good stuff, all of it. We may not like every experience we have and pray we never have to repeat them, but we learn from them, become better individuals because of them. All the crossroads we agonize over, they all eventually lead to the same place, they just expose us to different things along the way. Does it really matter if the people we meet and the experiences we have are on the streets of New York, at work, in church, in our own backyard or in a chemo ward? What matters is what we do with those experiences, how we embrace them and grow from them. Me, I am choosing to embrace them all and make them the best moments of my life.

They say that at any given moment, the experiences we are having are exactly the ones we are meant to have. For me, breast cancer may be one of the best experiences of my life. When I look past the physical component, which I do most of the time, there is so much more to it. We see ourselves in the mirror day after day, but do we really *see* ourselves? We spend a lifetime judging the physical image reflected back at us based on some standard we have created based on other people's opinions and norms, but with breast cancer, that is stripped away. Now, when I look in the mirror, I see a valuable human being smiling back at me. The physical body that hosts my soul is a vessel, one I can mimic the herd with or embrace as a canvas to express my own uniqueness. As I navigate the crossroads I am approaching, I choose the latter.

Breast cancer brings you intimately into relationship with yourself and with those closest to you. It releases you from the bonds of physical norms and allows you to explore who you really are. If you dare to be honest with yourself and those around you, you will blossom into the rarest and most beautiful of flowers. It is the blooming of the soul, and that, my friends, is a bloom that never fades.

Chapter 17 - More Trouble with Taxol

The trouble with Taxol is that there isn't a lot of trouble with Taxol, at least not for me. It has lulled me into a bizarre complacency, a "hey, this isn't so bad" state of mind. As I drift smugly down my twelve-week Taxol river, I have suddenly stopped counting the bends in the stream, stopped ticking off the weeks until the end. Maybe it's the Benadryl (I love to blame it on the Benadryl), but in my head, when I think of this phase of my chemo, I get a flash of me sipping a cocktail out of a coconut (okay, a lemonade out of a frosted glass) as I float down the gently meandering waters of a flower-lined stream on an inner-tube, having somehow won the chemo lottery. That has to be it, right? I won some sort of bizarre chemo lottery (thank you, whoever entered me) where I get to have a good experience instead of a bad one. Well, hold on to your piña coladas. The trouble with Taxol is that it sneaks up on you.

It's nothing major, just little pesky things, so small and inconsequential that you dismiss them like gnats at a picnic. How dare they ruin a perfect run. Well, they dare, so eventually you have to suck it up and deal with them. They are, in the grand scheme of things, still trivial, but they exist, and I would be remiss if I didn't own them.

1 - I'm possibly losing a fingernail. I know, right? One nail. The chemo class I took before I started my treatments said to use tea tree oil to combat that, but every time I swab it on my fingernails, they are sore the next morning. I'm three for three on the tea tree oil - sore fingers front, so I think we have a winner there. My nails aren't discolored or showing any signs of infection, although they have developed an interesting striated feel. When I'm feeling normal, I take a reality check by running my fingers over the new moon-like surface of my nails. It reminds me that the Taxol is sneaking up on me. Also, I used to have nice convex nails. Now, if you look at some of them at just the right angle, some of them look like they were mashed with a hammer. The top of the arch has sunken into little gullies. As for the one, the one possibly taking one for the team, it's still securely on, but half of my nail is white, giving me a gibbous moon nail rather than a nice, neat crescent moon of white at the tip. My toenails are all fine, but I do take care not to wear constricting shoes. So that's it, one nail. Personally, I think I owe it to myself. To make this experience whole, I should lose a nail. It's a small sacrifice to make.

2 - My nose. Not sure what's going on there, but I am not thrilled about it. After two months of post-nasal drip with phase one of my chemo, I thought I had moved back into blissful normalcy, aka no post-nasal drip. Then last week I felt like my sinuses were getting clogged, so I blew my nose and got what seemed like copious amounts of blood for my effort. Now, a week later, whenever I blow my nose, which is like every day, I get small pieces of skin that seem to have come loose from somewhere along with the blood. On the upside, I never get an actual nose bleed. I only see blood when I blow my nose. On the downside, it's moving into week two, and it's a side effect of the Taxol, so it's here to stay.

It's actually kind of funny when you think about it - I live in Florida, humidity central, and my sinuses are drying out. I'd take a hot shower and let the steam do its thing, but oh yeah, I can't put my hands or feet in hot water. Just so we have our bases covered, I've tried soothing my nasal passages with Neosporin on a Q-tip (my husband's trick) and used the saline spray they recommended in chemo class. Neither solve the problem, but they were both fun to try. I mean, what's not to like about sticking cotton soaked in goo up your nose or shooting a mist of salt water up your nose?

3 - My tongue. My tongue has started to look like the Grand Canyon, with deep ravines and crevices running across it. It is not painful, but it's not the most comfortable, either. It's more sensitive to, well, any food that has any flavor. I spend a lot of time swishing a mix of sea salt and baking soda around in my mouth. It helps, but I think this new landscape feature is also here to stay through the end of my Taxol treatment.

4 - Poison making its way out. There is no pretty way to say it except, after a while, the poison wants out. Sure, you pee it out, but the leftovers look for more creative exits. Most recently, it's making its way out through the pores on my face. Nope, not acne, this is different. Small white spots that come off with the barest scrape of a nail. It's also on my chest. It doesn't come off in the shower, it wants to be scraped off. It wants me to know it's there, to work for it.

Yes, that's the trouble with Taxol. In some respects, it is just like floating down a river. Just don't forget that river has a rocky bottom, so watch your butt poking through the inner tube. Don't ignore the warning signs, and don't forget to count the bends. Me, I have five more bends to go.

On the flip side, I have nothing to complain about. I am blessed beyond belief. They say if you have your health, you have everything. I have found that when your health is in question, you find out who is standing with you, waiting in the shadows to catch you should you stumble or fall. I'm a tough one to support. I am incredibly independent and self-reliant. Just know, I know you are there, wings spread wide, supporting me every step of the way. Just know I feel your breath on my neck, the kiss of encouragement, making each and every step along the way easier than the last. Just know, I love you all, and appreciate everything you do for me. The calls, the cards, the texts, the prayers, they are priceless to me.

Chapter 18 - It's All about the Breath

I'll admit it, I love to push my limits when I do yoga. It's my nature, I just can't shake that competitive urge, which is probably why lately, eight weeks into weekly chemo treatments, I run out of breath after the first Chair Pose. Enter Tao Porchon Lynch, the world's oldest yoga instructor at age ninety-eight. I was skating around Facebook in the wee hours of the morning on a post-chemo steroid buzz and ran across a post someone shared of her. Tao reminded me it's all about the breath, so I'm thinking this might be a great time for me to slow the burn and reconnect with *my* breath.

We hear it all the time in yoga, connect with the breath, but we rarely hear it in life. Breath is the life force that keeps us going. Inhale and we nourish our cells with life-ensuring oxygen; exhale and we get rid of carbon dioxide and all sorts of other cell waste, clearing the way for more life-affirming oxygen. So why don't we pay any attention to our breath? Is it because it's automatic? Our lungs faithfully inhale and exhale, changing the tempo as needed without our input or guidance? Much like our heart, they chug along doing their thing, until one day we notice something isn't quite right. Until one day, we are out of breath.

So I'm not saying I can't breathe, I'm saying it's time to give some love to one of the things I take for granted. I've always been fit, waltzing up the stairs at work without even a blip in my air intake. I mean, it's only one floor, what's the big deal? Until day by day, week by week, the waltz has become more of a climb, the handrail my only insurance against the possibility of a backslide instead of the expected forward motion. You would think I was climbing Mount Kilimanjaro, not one flight of stairs. Emerging from the stairwell, my lungs bellowing in and out in confusion, my brain not comprehending how one flight of stairs could possibly have that effect, I wonder how this has happened, how all of a sudden, without forewarning, my breath and I were strangers.

It seems like an odd concept, reconnecting with your breath. I like to see it more as reconnecting with your life force. In the bustle of day-to-day life, more and more of who we are gets pushed aside, supplanted by the outside world's clamor for attention. There was a time when at the end of the day we went home, took a deep breath, and reconnected. Some called it unwinding, often a glass of wine or a beer helped, but really we were reconnecting. We were shaking off the day and refocusing our attention on what really mattered, ourselves. Can we really even do that anymore, with smart phones and smart watches and Google glasses insisting that nothing be missed? The ever-present ring and ding of telephones and text messages and calendar notifications? Are we ever really free of the outside world's perpetual tug? How often do we do double duty, checking emails between bites of lunch or dinner? Our phones accompany us everywhere, for some even to the bathroom.

It's frightening when you think about it. That's why I long ago turned off all my email accounts on my cell phone. When I am not at a computer, there is nothing so important that I need to know about it right this instant. It can wait. The same goes for work. When I leave work, I leave it. When I get home, I am home. My home is not an extension of my work, it is an extension of me. I have reclaimed it one 100% as me territory. I have turned it back into the sanctuary it was always intended to be.

Back to the breath. I have boundaries, I have my sanctuary, so what's up with my breath? Time to reconnect my breath, my life force, with me. Since I do yoga, the easiest way for me to reconnect with my breath is through my yoga practice, to let my breath move me, physically, mentally, and spiritually, rather than being in reaction to it. Different yoga traditions do different things to accomplish that, but I am a basic kind of gal, so I reconnect with my breath by connecting it to movement without trying to manipulate it through ujjayi breathing. Put simply, I just connect every movement to an inhale or an exhale. One movement, one breath action. If I raise my arms overhead, that is an inhale, if I extend them out to the sides, that is an exhale. If I start to get winded, I stay in a pose for a few breaths until my lungs catch up.

It's all about connecting, and to connect, each part has to honor the other, remember how to dance together again until the rhythm of the parts becomes the rhythm of the one.

When I focus on moving with the breath, I find my practice is much slower and more mindful. It is easier to stay present in my poses without having to complicate them to keep me engaged. When I am connected with my breath, I find dynamic energy in all poses, not just the ones that challenge me physically. And, when I connect with the breath, I don't run out of air. When my physical movements are flowing with the breath, they are one, and one doesn't sap the other.

This is pretty much the yoga version of living in the moment. Instead of moving through a yoga practice, or any physical or mental modality for that matter, looking ahead to something more impressive and complicated to do with your mind or body, just enjoy the place you're in. Instead of running your body at full tilt until your lungs burst, marry the two, breath and body, and let them glide along together, one nourishing the other. I find, when I move with the breath, my lungs are open, I breathe more deeply, I don't have to struggle for air because air is always available. Long, deep, calming droughts of air are always moving in and out, in and out, in and out, and my mind, body, and spirit respond in kind. Much like if you cultivate a place of calm in your heart then calm is always available to you. When I find myself getting agitated, I just go sit by the pool of calm within me and it comes back. When I find my breath slipping away, I remember those long, deep, calming droughts of air that used to come so naturally and I smile, because I know that feeling is always available to me, and I'm not opposed to working for it.

Chapter 19 - A Perfect Day

What makes for a perfect day? For me, a perfect day is broken down into bite-size treasures of time, individual islands of experience that are destined to become cherished memories, all equally valuable, all equally precious. Quite often they are scraps of events, seemingly inconsequential. In the end, though, it is the staple spices, like black pepper or sea salt, that season the stew just right, and so it is with a perfect day. These scraps of time, sprinkled throughout the day, ensure that the day is spiced to remembrance.

I long ago stopped looking for the big wow to make my day and started focusing on the more commonplace events. My perfect day starts when I open my eyes and am greeted by the handsome sleeping form of my husband. I'm an early riser, so I get the delicious vantage point of admiring him while he sleeps. Sometimes I will snuggle close, putting my head on his shoulder and burying my nose in the soft skin of his neck. His arm wraps protectively around me when he feels me there, pulling me close so I can breathe in the delectable scent of him. Other days I just slip my hand quietly into his, reveling in the energy flowing through his fingers into mine, and mine into his. These moments are priceless to me. If the day were to end right there, it would be perfect! But the day is only beginning. There are innumerable more tidbits to come.

I like to start my day with yoga. That's not to say that sometimes I just don't feel like it, but perfection doesn't necessarily mean I want to, it often means that I do it anyway. So, like it or not, I get on the mat. With chemo, as of late, this has become harder and harder. My energy does not rebound as quickly as it used to and the Energizer Bunny in me seems to be running on old batteries much of the time, but getting on the mat is usually 99% of the battle, so I plant myself in the middle of my mat, cross-legged, and begin some light stretching to feel things out. If nothing else, stretching everything out is always a boon, plus I usually have a hand free to scratch Jill, my cat.

Jill has a starring role in a good deal of my perfect day moments, probably because her timing is impeccable. Just this morning she planted herself on the end of my mat and did a half-body roll to expose a snowy white chest for scratching. She never does that; she's more of a neck gal, but I went with it and scratched her chest and under her arms while she stretched them languidly overhead, encouraging me to try for the tucked-away places. It's a simple thing, really, to take a moment to scratch the cat, to find that one place where she goes, "Yeah, baby, that's the spot," but it means the world to me, that roaring purr of happiness. It perfects my day. Plus, she makes my yoga more fun, more inspired. Anybody can muscle through a yoga practice when their mat is their own. When you share your mat with a cat, creativity takes over and you are inspired toward a more playful, graceful practice, rather than one too adherent to any structure or focus. You must be willing to change your flow on a dime, butt heads with aplomb, and rub your face in copious amounts of fur, but it is oh so worth it!

After yoga comes meditation. When I was diagnosed with breast cancer, I started meditating to clear out the emotional garbage I was holding on to. Now, I meditate to bring in the wonders of the universe. For me, it is a time to give thanks for the blessings in my life and to listen to the whispering of the cosmos. It's magical, really, the wisdom that is out there for the listening. For me, this sagacity comes more in the form of reminders; they are things I already know but have pushed aside for whatever reason. Through meditation, they are whispered back into the forefront so I can incorporate them back into my life again. There usually isn't anything complicated about them—embrace joy, peace, hope; invite balance into my life; release anger, frustration, fear; practice yoga; meditate; be creative; write. They are simple things, things I do already, but the universe knows when one is slipping out of whack and whispers her reminder to me to pay attention, be mindful there. I think of it as a cosmic tap on the shoulder, perfect in every way.

From here, the day can go pretty much anywhere. Last Saturday was a perfect Saturday. I spent the day in the hammock my husband bought me for my birthday (it is awesome!) nestled in pillows and blankets, reading a book. I was feeling a little weak and so it fit the bill. Friday was also a perfect day—I went to work. You see, it doesn't matter what I'm doing that defines the day as perfect, it is being fully engaged in what I'm doing. If I work and relax in equal measures, that's perfection! If one takes over, skewing the recipe, then resentment builds up and I feel the pull of the other, whether it is work or play. Balance is the key here. A healthy balance of work and personal time leads to a perfect day, day after day after day!

One other thing I do every day is I speak with my mother. It wasn't always this way, but I am forever grateful that the stars realigned to connect us in such a deep and meaningful way. It's not that we talk about anything earth-shattering—she tells me what she's doing that day, or fills me in on a lecture or event she attended the day before. I tell her what I'm up to, how I'm feeling, what the day has in store. These conversations are the threads that bind us, that keep us close and involved in one another's lives, erasing the miles between us. And sometimes, like today, I call again in the evening just to hear her voice. Sometimes, when you have cancer and you don't feel as great as you would like to, your mother's voice makes it all better. It's chicken soup for a child's soul. It's, well, Mom.

So there you have it, the recipe for a perfect day. Tomorrow I have chemo, another perfect day in the making. Seasoned with activities that inspire me, sparkling with people I love, adventure awaits with new nurses to meet, familiar faces to greet, fresh stories to hear, and of course, a treatment to take that brings me that much closer to a cancer-free life. Onward ho! Adventure, here I come!

Chapter 20 - Baby, It's Cold Outside

We are in a cold dip here in sunny Central Florida. It is what passes for winter in the Sunshine State, delightful weather occasionally punctuated with cold spells of fifty-degree days and thirty- to forty-degree nights. When you are used to perpetual variations of warm weather, it can be a shock to the system. When your blood is limping through your veins and you are running on low-test, the cold feels, well, colder. To the normal world, like say, my cat, she wants to go outside and enjoy the rare brisk weather, but I am having no part of it. Letting her out isn't the issue; it's that she wants the door to stay open in case the boogeyman appears and she needs to beat a hasty retreat into the sanctuary of the house. Baby, it's cold outside, and I don't want it inside.

As my Taxol treatments stretch on, as is to be expected, my blood is stretching thin along with it. With Taxol, every week, a little bit, a little bit, your blood count takes two steps back, one step forward. So here I am, nine weeks in, and the shuffle is butting up against my comfort zone, and I'm cold. It's a bone-chilling cold that seems to emanate from inside me, frosting my organs on its way to my fingers and toes. What is left of the hair on my arms now stands perpetually on end, fixed in some sort of mock attention, waiting for a command of "at ease" that, from where I sit, will likely be a long time coming. My core, rather than being a heat source, feels like spent ash. The ember is in there somewhere, I am certain of it, but I'm not quite sure how to get at it, how to coax it back to life. It feels dormant, vacant, like it has suddenly decided to sit the rest of this chemo thing out and bugged out for warmer digs. It is not hard to imagine my core sunning itself on a warm beach somewhere, penning a postcard that says only, "Call when it's safe to come home." If I could, I would likely do the same. But I can't.

One of the interesting things about being chemo cold is how different it feels and acts from being regular old cold. I tried jump-starting a little core heat by riding my spin bike. Nothing crazy, just a nice light ride around New Zealand (BitGym—awesome running-walking-biking app!) It didn't work. Even with a space heater pointed at me blasting on high and wearing a thermal shirt and a sweatshirt, I barely reached comfortable. On the upside, New Zealand is gorgeous, so if nothing else, I got to escape for a brief time to someplace where it actually was warm. Yoga is also good for generating core heat, but these days my yoga is gentle and the only heat being generated is by the aforementioned space heater. With a little more oomph I could pull it off, but I promised a slew of people I wouldn't overdo things, so my heat-generating capabilities lag behind the creep of the cold at this point. For me, for now, baby, I'm cold inside.

So here's a fun fact: when your fingers are under the influence of Taxol, not too numb, but in that slightly deadened place where it feels like your fingertips are calloused, or like you are touching everything through latex gloves, when they reach a certain state of too cold, if you tap your fingertips just right, the nerves will act like a tuning fork and the sound of the touch will vibrate inside your finger. Okay, it did scare the heck out of me when it first happened, but once I got past that, it was pretty darn cool.

Then, there are the nights. I sleep in flannel pajamas with socks on under a comforter with three blankets piled on top of that. Then, and only then, am I comfortable enough to fall asleep. Take one blanket away and I get a chill and wake up. Add the warmth of the cat in all her purring glory, heaven! My husband curls up next to me with just a sheet. Add anything more and he is drenched in sweat. Last night we put the heat on seventy degrees and I still slept under all those blankets. It's like I have lost the ability to generate my own body heat. I've never been someone who runs hot anyway, but this is taking it to a new, dare I say, low.

I have three more treatments, so I am preparing myself for a lengthy cold spell. I try not to daydream about hot, steaming bathtubs frosted with scented bubbles. I don't think hot water is in the cards for me anytime soon, as the heat sensitivity can last for some time after the last treatment. I used to love hot baths. Really, really hot baths, ringed in candles, the scent of vanilla or brown sugar wafting on the steam ... Darn! I wasn't going to do that.

I suspect this is what is meant by collateral damage, the things I will give up in the hopes of a cancer-free future. I also suspect that when all is said and done, I won't miss these castaways at all. The human body, mind, and spirit are incredibly resilient. They accept, incorporate, and move on. I can't say I will ever really like the cold, but I suspect I will not miss scalding showers so much, or hot baths. They will slip away like so many other old favorites that have followed the same path in my lifetime, replaced by something contemporary that fits this time and space more uniquely. Like a hammock, and the tickle of a waft of wind on my face as I enjoy the delicious blend of sun and breeze on any number of perfect Florida afternoons. What I will keep forever is what really matters. The cards from Connie, my mother-in-law, sending her love and prayers; the memories of phone calls, texts, and blog comments connecting me to friends and family; the love and constancy of my amazing husband; the purr of a devoted companion. These things nothing can take away from me, not even cancer.

Chapter 21 - It Takes a Village

Another Thursday, another Taxol treatment. Only two more to go and then I'm done with chemo. It's bittersweet, this drawing to a close of this chapter of my life. I will miss them, my village of people who welcome me into their fold on chemo day and make sure it is as amazing as I make it out to be. I'm pretty sure it really is. I've been through fourteen treatments so far, and each time I am not disappointed. Each time, I come away feeling loved and cared for, and that much closer to being cancer-free.

I will miss the security guards that check me into the building with kindness and grace, honoring my humanity and the reason I am there. They always have a kind word, and some even bravely ask a question or two. How strange I must seem, marching in with my cooler of frozen peas and bag stuffed with blankets and snacks, as though I were headed for some bizarre daytime slumber party.

I will miss the staff at the front desk in the lobby. When Ken and I arrive, they greet us like old friends on the way in and send us off with well wishes when we pass them again on the way out. I suppose in many ways we are old friends, having seen one another weekly for more than two months in addition to having spent time together on tours of the Cancer Center. Ken and I went on a tour as part of the chemo class before my treatments started, and when my mother came to visit at Christmas, I set up a special tour for her so she could see for herself where her baby goes for chemo, or "where the magic happens," as I like to say, to put her at ease and give her peace of mind that I am in excellent hands. I joined them for that tour as well. So yes, we are indeed old friends, the very best of old friends.

I will miss the people I run into in the elevator, their smiles and easy chatter. Some are going to the same floor, some are venturing higher to offices or doctor's appointments, or maybe just visiting. Regardless, we share a common goal, a common thread, and that binds us for that brief ride, then releases us back to our lives having been enriched by the encounter.

I will miss the ladies at the front desk at 5LP, the outpatient chemo floor at the UF Health Cancer Center. I will miss their laughter, their easy comfort with their roles as the keepers of people's worst fears - what comes next. Whatever magical DNA they possess, the occupants wait at ease, reading magazines, chatting easily among themselves, and laughing with the nurses when they come in to fetch them, signaling it's their turn for some one-on-one pampering. We all know what is coming next, and it is not scary. It is a necessary evil, delivered with kindness and compassion by highly skilled nurses who will do all they can to ensure we are comfortable and feel cared for.

I will miss the nurses. Up until now, I have had a different nurse each week. It's how the scheduling falls. Patient treatment times vary, so they fit them together like a massive multi-level jigsaw puzzle, matching treatment lengths to time slots to nurses. Mine is relatively short, I'm in and out in two and a half hours, but some are there for half a day or longer. Regardless, each nurse is a jewel in my sixteen-strand necklace called chemo. For the last three weeks, I have had the same nurse, Meredith. She is wonderful. She has an easy laugh and we chat about symptoms and how to mitigate them as though they were clouds and a puff of breath is all it would take to move them on and produce a sunny day. With her, it is that easy, it is that comfortable. When I leave, we hug, sending each other on to the rest of our day with a warm, fuzzy feeling, which for me has nothing to do with the Benadryl or the Taxol.

I will miss the artwork on the walls. It is everywhere on the chemo floor and throughout the hospital. Most of it has been done by patients as part of the Healing Arts program at the Cancer Center. An artist comes to the chemo floor and works with patients while they are receiving treatment, or you can sign up for any number of classes that take place in the Support Community Clubhouse, from drawing to painting, knitting and crocheting, writing, yoga, meditation, tai chi ... the list seems endless. Or, attend any number of support groups. I used to avoid this section of the hospital, the Support Community Clubhouse. I am happy, why taint that with people who quite possibly are not happy in their process? Then I remembered that these communities work both ways, that it is the mix of people, some grieving their diagnosis and some celebrating their process, that makes the community whole, helps it heal, so I have dipped my toe in and joined a journaling class. I am finding it very rewarding to interact with others, honoring each of our place in our own process and offering words of encouragement where we can.

One of the exercises during the first class was to write about a word from a list the instructor provided. I chose the word "lake." Here is what I wrote:

> *Clear, still water kisses the edge of reality. It toys with different versions of itself, mixing slowly, belly side up, belly side up, modeling different facades, never quite content with what it sees.*

> *Plop! A stone skips across the surface - one, two, three times - shattering the illusion of a perfect day.*

> *Disturbed, waves claw the shore, grasping for a new reality. Belly side up, belly side up, what face comes next. Who will I be today? Who ...*

For me, and since I wrote it I'm comfortable taking a stab at the meaning, it's about the process of having breast cancer. The ever-shifting sands, or water in this case, of diagnosis, treatment, and beyond. Of gathering information, getting comfortable with a potential future outcome, then new information comes to light and shatters the new future you have come to accept, sending you scrambling back to square one. In time, the entire process takes on a matter-of-fact comfort of its own. The shattering and re-acceptance become a game, one where you try on new physical, and corresponding emotional, versions of yourself until you find one you are comfortable with, only to have them upended and you start over. But you know that. You know that planning your physical future when you are in treatment for breast cancer is ludicrous. Still, you play the game. It is comforting in a convoluted way. Like waves on the shoreline, a momentary kiss on an ever-changing reality is better than none at all.

Finally, I will miss the time I spend with my husband. Chemo is a very intimate time, like it or not. Once a week, my husband gets to see me at my most vulnerable, and I get to see him at his strongest. He is unwavering. I know, I can see it in his eyes, in his demeanor, in his every action. He is there by my side, at the ready, to do and be what I need. When we get to chemo, he tenderly unpacks my bag. He lays my blanket over me and arranges my water and toast on the side table. Then he puts three mints out for me in case I need them for the port flushes, which have a tendency to leave a salty alcohol taste in my mouth. Later, when I am half asleep and unsure of what is going on, he will make sure the cookie lady leaves an oatmeal raisin cookie for me so I will have it when I wake up. He is my rock.

They say it takes a village to raise a child, well, it takes a village to get chemo. This is my village, and I am grateful for them all. This is my village, and I will miss them.

Chapter 22 - Gratitude, It's an Attitude

I get asked all the time, how I can have such a positive attitude when I have cancer? To me, really, how can I not? I go to and leave chemo with a smile on my face, laughter in my heart, and a sense that all is right in the world, because for me, all is right in the world. Things are exactly as they should be. How could they be otherwise? In this moment, right now, this is where I reside, and so this is the most wonderful, the most precious, point in time. This moment is perfect, just as it is.

It is bandied around, this concept of an "attitude of gratitude." What is it really? For me, it is just being grateful. It is crowding out the negative thoughts with their better halves, their steadfast, stalwart counterparts who too often become the unsung heroes in our lives. They are there, these happy moments, waiting patiently on the sidelines to be noticed and celebrated, so I choose to bring them forward, day in and day out, and make them the centerpieces of my existence. I choose to be grateful for the good in my life, rather than moon over, well, anything else. Sure, I have my moments, but I don't dwell on them. I choose the other side of the coin; I choose gratitude.

Listen. Do you hear it? It could be anything ... the song of a bird, the tinkle of a wind chime, the hum of crickets, or maybe the playful, throaty staccato of tree frogs. Beautiful, aren't they? Let them in! Quiet the voices in your head, the negative drone of discontent, and let the songs of nature in. Let them rumble around in there; let them take up space. The glorious, carefree sounds of life in all its glory are all around us. Let these happy sounds become the new theme songs of your life.

Look. Do you see it? It could be anything ... a flower in bloom, sunlight filtering through the leaves, dappling the ground in a kaleidoscope of patterns, a parade of fluffy white shapes drifting across the sky, changing on a dime for your amusement alone.

Beautiful, aren't they? I spend a lot of time watching the clouds these days. I have a perfect vantage point from the comfort of our hammock. Oddly, winged pigs fly around my house a lot, charging out of the cloud banks, snouts held high, wings spread wide for the next downward swoosh that will propel them across the sky to the safety of the next cloud bank. And sometimes, when they don't know I'm looking, I can see angel wings peeking out from behind the clouds. I know they are watching over me, but it's nice to know that their curiosity sometimes gets the better of them too and they peek out a little too far, giving us down below a flash of cottony white wing.

Keep going. Breathe in the smells ... of plants, of cooking, of your home, of your family. It's glorious! This nose we have, it takes it all in. Let it register, let it inspire you. My favorite time of year is when the tea olive bush is blooming in our backyard. I love walking out onto the back patio on a summer day and being surprised by the sudden wash of scent that has, seemingly overnight, taken over to surprise me. I can't breathe it in deep enough. It's intoxicating! Then again, so is the scent of my husband, and the scent of Jill, my cat. I love to bury my nose in both of their necks and breathe in their scents. To me, they are what love smells like.

Now, feel it. I have a hard time letting all that in, the sights, the sounds, the smells, without feeling overwhelming gratitude. Gratitude for the body I have that lets me experience all these things; gratitude for this world I live in where all these things are always around me, there for the experiencing, if I just stop, for a moment, and notice them. If I just let them in.

So, back to the cancer thing. Am I grateful I have cancer? In some ways, yes. It has opened me up to some amazing experiences, connected me with some amazing people, brought me closer to the people I love. It has allowed me to be vulnerable in a very healthy way, and let me grow in strength in an equally healthy way. More so now than ever, I realize I have spent my whole life knowing if I had just slowed down, had just looked left, or right, or up, or even down, there would have been something amazing there, but I was too engrossed with what lay ahead. I was too engrossed in things that, quite frankly, didn't matter. Well, now I know better. I know that forward is a direction, but the good stuff is all around me in the here and now. I know that before tomorrow comes, there is this amazing, glorious thing called today. I know that the only thing that matters is right now. Tomorrow, and the next day, and the next day after that, will come soon enough, and when they do, they will have their time to shine, but for right now, this moment has my undivided attention, and it is magnificent!

Chapter 23 - Taxol Can Be a Sneaky Bunkmate

Taxol has turned out to be a sneaky companion on this adventure. What started out as a mild, hazy muddle of weekly treatments with no real downside, or upside, or, well, sides at all, rapidly reached a sucker-punched state right around week nine, when my nurse informed me that my white blood count was getting too low and the next week I would likely have to either miss a treatment or get a Nupigen shot to boost my white blood cell production. After having gone through four Neulasta shots in phase one of my chemo, one after every bi-weekly infusion, my PTNOS flared up (Post Traumatic Neulasta Onpro Syndrome, which my nurse tells me is indeed a real thing!) at the thought of an injection that was any relative of Neulasta. While Neulasta is, and was, extremely helpful in stimulating my bone marrow to produce blood cells of all kinds on overdrive, it really, well, sucked.

So here is how Neulasta Onpro works. Right after chemo, they put the Neulasta Onpro on your arm. You know the one, the commercials are everywhere. The happy-go-lucky cancer patients are going about their happy-go-lucky lives with this flashing alien pod stuck to the back of their arm, not a care in the world, because Neulasta Onpro is counting down their twenty-seven hours of happy-go-luckiness before the crap hits the fan. Oh, yes, counting down, or shall I say, flashing down. Flash, flash, flash ... because when hour twenty-seven hits, the flashing stops and the clicking starts. The click of injection, which takes forty-five minutes, by the way. You don't actually feel it, the needle has been in your arm for twenty-seven hours. It embedded itself there three minutes after they stuck the Onpro on your arm. Sometimes you can feel the needle go in (barely half an inch long, by the way) which feels like someone snapped the back of your arm with a rubber band, and since you have a pod stuck there, no, you can't rub it to make it feel better. You get to smile and move on, thrilled it's there, because that means you don't have to come back twenty-seven hours later for a physical shot, but still muttering, "Damn, that stings." I was lucky on this front, I only felt it one out of the four times. Anyway, it's the injection that does the psychological damage. For me, for forty-five minutes I heard the click, click, clicking of the drug slowly seeping into my body, and with each click-drip my face would get redder and I would get hotter. After forty-five minutes, the pod beeps to tell you the damage is done, the payload is delivered, your next seven days will be hell. You are now free to remove the Onpro, and oh, have a nice week.

Ah, getting it off, now that's fun too. It's glued to your arm, intended to be water, or drug, tight, with a needle embedded in your arm. It's a two-man job. Thank God for Ken.

Yes, seven days of hell. Bone ache, which I was lucky enough to only have for the first round, but that was enough for me. I woke up at four in the morning feeling like I had suddenly developed advanced arthritis in my hands somewhere between bedtime and my painful wake-up call. An Allegra knocked it out, but it was indeed a wake-up call, in more ways than one. Within two to three days, the flu-like symptoms started - runny nose, achy, slight fever. I say flu-like because I got to have all the symptoms without actually having the flu. Strangely, there was some solace in it, feeling flu-ish but knowing I wasn't really sick. Then, like a phoenix from the ashes, around day eight I would wake up and feel fine, like none of it ever happened and it was just a bad dream. Then the next week comes and I got this feeling of dread, and it wasn't about the chemo. My body hated it, the Neulasta Onpro. Something else goes on inside you with the Neulasta. I can't put my finger on it, but my body knows, and it doesn't want it. PTNOS doesn't lie.

Funny story, or not so funny, depending on how you look at it. My bread maker died the week after I finished up my first phase of chemo and my last Neulasta Onpro injection. I replaced it with a Cuisinart bread maker. Awesome machine, but imagine my surprise when I test drove it with a loaf of cinnamon raisin bread and heard a faint, but familiar, clicking sound as it went through its paces. I had to search my body for an Onpro to quell the anxiety, convince myself it wasn't true, that there wasn't one injecting into me. I contemplated sending the machine back, but in the end it has been good therapy. I can't go through life going into a panic every time something clicks in a high, whimsical pitch. Still, it is thirteen weeks later and I still have a moment when I hear that clicking start. Don't underestimate the body's aversion to Neulasta Onpro.

So back to the real story. There I was in week nine with three weeks to go and the possibility of a Neulasta-like injection in my future, and I started to panic. Me in panic mode - get answers. I grilled my chemo nurse, called my doctor, even broke my cardinal rule of not using the Internet to find solutions, to no avail. It seems that there are no foods or supplements that stimulate white blood cell production (Taxol only lowers your white blood cell count, the rest are fine). Ken was convinced that steak would help, the nurse said leafy greens are good for you, so I decided to just wing it. We had steak one night, I added spinach to my smoothies, I went to sleep earlier, and I was more diligent with my exercise and meditation, even taking a few more turns on the spin bike. In the end, it couldn't hurt.

So, like I said, Taxol is sneaky, but my body, apparently, has a trick or two left up its Onpro-less sleeve as well. Each week, for nine weeks, the Taxol had been eroding my white blood cell count. Slowly, slowly, it, and I, had been fading, until I felt like a cold, hollow, ashy being. Then, like a phoenix from the ashes, the blood work for my tenth chemo session came back that my white cell count had gone up! My nurse, Meredith, was as excited as I was. No more two steps back, one step forward. I had moved on to a new dance, one step back, two steps forward! I was dumbfounded, and excited, but mostly dumbfounded. After nine weeks of a certain pattern, you get flabbergasted when for no apparent reason it suddenly changes. This week was my eleventh chemo session, and my blood work came back again that my white cell count had gone up. That's two weeks in a row! Needless to say, I'm ecstatic about this sudden turn of events. With only one more chemo session left to go, I'm certain I won't be skipping a treatment or getting a Nupigen shot.

Who's to say why these things happen. Maybe my body just finally responded to my meditations and affirmations. Maybe the PTNOS stimulated some primitive self-preservation response in my body and it did the impossible, it turned the *Titanic* and avoided an imminent collision with a short needle and misery. Maybe the angels threw my body some side eye, a sort of "get with the program, only a few more weeks" incentive. I suppose I'll never know, but like always, I'm grateful for whatever happened. Really, really grateful.

It's the small things in life that often make the biggest difference. So, thank you to everyone who said a prayer, whispered a thought, is rooting for me, reads my blog, is reading this book, smiles at the content, forwards it to a friend, wonders how I'm doing, wonders who I am, or just wonders. All these thoughts, they come together, they have energy and power, more than we will ever know. All these thoughts, in some way, helped to turn this *Titanic*, and I am grateful, very grateful, so thank you. Together, we out-sneaked the Taxol.

Chapter 24 - Chemo Is a Crooked Road

After sixteen treatments, my chemo is done. Yeah! Right? Maybe not. Cancer is a crooked road, and chemo is only one leg of the journey. Chemo was not too bad, relatively speaking, but what lies ahead, that is the great unknown.

I went into chemo with a lot of trepidation, although acknowledging it was the best course of treatment for my situation. After all my tests were done, there was a lymph node that came back positive for cancer cells. In order to potentially reduce the number of lymph nodes that might have to be removed during surgery, I elected to go through a course of chemo to hopefully kill any cancer cells lurking there. It wasn't ideal, but I decided that short-term discomfort during chemo would make more sense than increasing my chances of potential permanent physical issues post-surgery. It worked out in the sense that the chemo was not the horror show that the movies make it out to be. Oncologists have gotten exceptionally good at mitigating the downside of chemo. Towards the end, it started to catch up to me. The Energizer Bunny effect has faded and I'm more of a droopy hound dog these days, but it's over and done with and I'm sure I'll bounce back in no time.

Chemo is a crooked road, though, and oddly, I found myself growing fond of my weekly infusions. There was a certain comfort in the routine, especially during Taxol, which was twelve weeks long. While I was in chemo, in the back of my mind was always the thought that each treatment was encouraging the cancer cells to die, so as long as I was getting treated, the cancer was in retreat, so to speak. Since the very first treatment, way back in November, the tumor has steadily shrunk, so what's not to like? The more it shrinks, the greater the chances of, well, something good, right? So here I am, at the end of my crooked chemo road, and the overwhelming emotion is sadness.

Try as I might, and I've tried, I can't figure out what I have to be sad about. Yes, there is the change in routine; yes, I will miss the staff and nurses on LP5, the outpatient chemo floor; and yes, no more chemo! I would think the no-more-chemo would outrank the rest, the idea that the poisoning has stopped and I can start to recover. That my hair will grow back and my fingernails will stop hurting, my nose will stop bleeding and my face will stop flaking. I'll grow eyebrows and eyelashes again, and stop having to worry about white blood cell counts and the density of the crowd. It all seems small in the face of what comes next, though. These known inconveniences have a comfort level to them, a known commodity that is unwavering, week after week. What comes next is new and scary, and honestly, most likely really, really painful. I had a breast biopsy as part of my investigative tests and it was excruciatingly painful. I can't fathom the pain that comes with a lumpectomy or a mastectomy.

I'm not usually one to shy away from pain. It is what it is, so to speak. I've been on this cancer road for eight months now, and it hasn't gotten any less crooked. What comes next lurks behind a bend in the road, unavailable for scrutiny until that section of road has been rounded. That will likely be a week from Tuesday, when I meet with my oncologist and surgeon post-MRI. The MRI will tell them the size of the tumor after the chemo and the next stage of my journey will begin to unfold. I have tried not to think about it, the options that are not options without more information, but it is hard not to. There can be, after all, just so many options, or so I think, from where I sit. That's why it's better not to think about it, because I don't have all the options, or the answers, or even the information to figure out the options or the answers. It is best, for now, to just enjoy the last stretch of crooked road I am familiar with, until I round the bend.

Yesterday was a perfect hammock day. The sky was overcast, so I snuggled into a nest of blankets and pillows and read a book and enjoyed the sky. At one point, a perfect smiley face accompanied by a cartoon dog face—long nose sniffing about the sky and floppy ears askew—smiled down at me in tandem, confirming the day was as perfect as it seemed. In response, I turned my sad face upside down and smiled back.

A potpourri of birds stopped off in the yard, skipping along the fence tops and scampering about in the grass. One cannot stay sad for long watching their happy dances. Cardinals, wrens, starlings, even an American bluebird, all taking a break from their busy day to encourage a smile from me. Even Jill, my cat, found them entertaining and chirped along with them from the confines of the pool enclosure as they dashed about.

I never cease to be amazed by the healing power of nature. Sadness can come, but is just as easily chased away by a smiley face-shaped cloud and a flock of birds. Yes, cancer is a crooked road, but nature, I have come to find, grows alongside that road, accompanying me every step of the way. She is always on hand to lift my spirits, to pick me up and dust me off, to remind me that together we can face the bend in the road. When sadness comes sniffing around, all I need to do is look up, look around, look within, and soon enough, I'll be smiling again.

Chapter 25 - Giving a Goblin a Makeover

It has taken a while to get the goo of disgruntlement off of me since my post about Neulasta Onpro (*Chapter 23 - Taxol Can Be a Sneaky Bunkmate*). It is one of the reasons I prefer not to go negative, it's so darn hard to feel fresh again. Amid the onslaught of discouraging thoughts that pervade our daily lives, we are too often left to ourselves to coax out our own smile, to find our own patch of white snow amid the ashen detritus that too often lines the roads of our lives. That is why I find it easier to live in a happy place and eschew the temptation of a black thought, because going around a tar pit will forever be easier than climbing back out of one once you have soaked yourself in its muddy bottom.

I saw a goblin staring down at me from the clouds yesterday. Pointy eared and firm of gaze, he watched, emotionless, waiting for me to label him. It would have been easy to call him a miscreant, letting folklore be the definer and going with the proverbial flow, but no. His edges softening under the encouragement of the breeze that had molded him, I decided to imagine him otherwise. He may have been, for that brief moment, a goblin, but deep down he was still a cloud, destined to become whatever my imagination chose to discern.

So why a goblin? I could dismiss it as the leftover splatter of Neulasta discontent. Much like gum on a shoe, gloominess sticks around longer than it should, rebuffing any kind of mandated expiration date to remind us it's still lurking about when we least expect it. Instead, I shall ask, why not a goblin? It's not the goblin that prompts the malcontent; in truth, it is my need to cast off this recent spate of negative emotions on the first external embodiment I can find that has summoned this poster child for the thoughts and feelings I am apparently desperate to rid myself of. At least desperate enough to conjure up a goblin as my fall guy. Yes, there it is, the eternal ray of sunshine is having cloudy thoughts. I have officially entered what I am told is Phase II of the grieving process.

Yes, grief. Apparently, breast cancer is a grief journey. Who knew? Me, I skipped off on an adventure, and little did I know it was into the lion's den. And, although as of late I am not as blissfully happy as I have been heretofore, which I could also blame on the abrupt cessation of my weekly dose of steroids and Benadryl, I am not exactly melting into a puddle of uncontrollable tears and anguish either. I'd say I was behaving hormonally, but that's a biological impossibility, so likely not. No, I am entering "Phase II," having skipped Phase I entirely, or having simply failed to notice it. As for my goblin friend, I will admire his pointy ears one last time as they fade into wisps. His work is done.

I watch the clouds because they are a reflection of my inner self, a mirror held up to my subconscious. The images, they are the calling cards of my psyche popping out for tea and a chat. Sometimes it's good flying weather and winged pigs abound, and sometimes a goblin, front and center, staring expectantly, prodding me to choose a side, elect a state of mind from which my perception of the sky and its banal white clouds will reveal my innermost secrets.

I've tried to take pictures of the Rorschach clouds that cavort around the skies for me, to no avail. It's a little like taking a photo of a thought. I can capture the cloud, but when I look at it any time later, it is just a puff of cotton, meaningless, the interpretation having long become obsolete. It is better to enjoy the clouds while they happen, when the prod is relevant, and act upon them accordingly. For me, for now, while I am still scraping gum off my shoe, the gloom has become less sharp. It has faded to gray wisps and is hopefully making its way to join the white bits of clouds that have called it out. Meanwhile, I will explore this new thing in my life called Grief - Phase II. An adventure awaits, and I am never one to shy away from an adventure.

Chapter 26 - Remember to Bring a Flashlight

Thursday, February 16, 2017, was my last chemo treatment. My doctors and nurses were really good at managing what they term the side effects of chemo (and what I call effects, because let's call a spade a spade, everything that happens during chemo is an effect of chemo), but they have pretty much left me to my own devices to sort out the aftermath of being cut off from my weekly dose of Benadryl and steroids. A quick buzz around the Internet shows nothing regarding palliative chemo care withdrawal. I suppose it is a small price to pay, and minor league in terms of the real collateral damage some patients suffer, so I thought I'd make a list of the inconveniences that set in when you are coming out of treatment for anyone else going through chemo and wondering what might happen next.

The first week was fine, but when Thursday rolled around again, my usual chemo day, the proverbial shit hit the fan. This is my post-chemo experience after twelve weeks of Taxol and sixteen total chemo treatments:

1 - **Pissed off** - after being plied with drugs that relax, sedate and stimulate you, respectively, and by the way, stay in your system for quite a while after administered, you wake up one day pretty darn irritated. I don't take medications as a rule. I have to really, really need them to go there, so being steadily medicated for four and a half months is new for me, new for my body, and new for people I interact with. Getting off that ride wasn't pretty. Once the time for my usual dosing passed, I could feel my fuse getting shorter, and shorter, and shorter. Add to that Friday was one of those days when everything that could go wrong went wrong, at least from my newly incensed perspective, I think I did a pretty good job not letting the bats out of the belfry. The better news is my unpleasant state of mind didn't last long. By Saturday afternoon I felt the pall of fury lift. I did have a meltdown Saturday morning

though, much to the chagrin of my husband, Ken. (Nothing to do with him, he just had ringside seats.)

2 - **Muscle stiffness** - my muscles have been stiff for weeks now. I'm thinking a cumulative Benadryl overdose, which muscle stiffness is a symptom of. I'm not surprised, since I've been dosed with the drug for twelve weeks straight. They say it comes out of your body pretty quickly and by the following day it is gone, but I found a study that begs to differ. It's a bummer, really, since in the beginning the Benadryl had the delightful side effect of making me really loose, letting me get into yoga poses I had previously just scratched my head in wonder over. Now, I can barely do a forward fold without my hamstrings screaming and threatening to rip. The most prevalent pain is in my jaw, which has ached for the past several weeks. It comes and goes, which is nice, but just when I think it may have moved on for good, it's back. Nuts. (And yes, I've mentioned this "effect" to my nurses and doctor, who just looked puzzled. Leave it to me to be over-Benadryl-ed.)

Side note - come to find out that it is more likely the Prednisone, or lack thereof, that is causing the feeling of muscle stiffness, since it was the Prednisone that made my muscles really loose in the first place. Another reason not to self-diagnose with the Internet. Chances are you will get it wrong.

3 - **Dry mouth** - considering what I went through with the first phase of my chemo (lips sticking to my teeth, waking up every two hours with my eyeballs glued to my eyelids), this is mild, but I still have a dry mouth that prevents me from sleeping through the night, or for any duration of time for that matter. The upside is I don't drool while I sleep; there isn't enough moisture in my mouth to accomplish that. My mouth is on constant drought watch, though, and wakes me up every three to four hours with a thirst alert.

4 - **Itching** - this is new, and not so fun, since it is impossible to scratch anything effectively with my newly unimproved post-Taxol nails. To recap, Taxol attacks the nail bed and causes your fingernail to lift from your finger. It also increases the chances of

fungal infections under your nails. While I didn't lose any fingernails to Taxol or get any fungal infections, most of them have some nail bed damage, so the white section on the tip of my nail has expanded to encompass about one-fifth to one-quarter of my nail. It is unnoticeable to the untrained eye, but I don't want to catch my nails on anything or stress them in any way lest they pull up or tear off. They are actually pretty sturdy, but I've come this far, so I'm not taking any chances. Back to itching, the bottoms of my feet have started itching, and my back, and my thighs, and my palms, and my head. You get the picture, random bouts of itching anywhere on my body that I can't scratch effectively.

5 - **Hungry, yet full, yet hungry** - pretty self-explanatory. I'm hungry, but I feel full. My appetite center is confused, very confused. I have tried eating anyway, but then I just feel too full. I'm trying to stymie the effect by eating soft foods that will sit easily, like scrambled eggs with mixed vegetables (broccoli, cauliflower and green beans) and cheddar cheese mixed in. I can eat more of that than say something heavier, like chicken. Hmmm ... chicken tacos sound good right about now. Like I said, I'm hungry, always hungry, but I'm full.

6 - **Fatigue** - I'm tired. Somewhat physically tired, but mostly emotionally tired. I navigated my chemo with minimal absence from work. For the twelve weeks of Taxol, I took the day of chemo off and worked full time the other four days. I think I called in sick twice over the full twenty weeks. From this side of treatment, it made sense, because the tiring part is now, after chemo. Right now, I could use at least a week off to recover and regroup. Food for thought for all of you planning your treatment, or with friends planning treatment. After chemo is more tiring than chemo will ever be.

I would be remiss if I didn't follow up my angst list with some post-chemo wins. My fingernails are no longer sore, and little sprouts of hair are making an appearance. I lost about ten pounds during chemo (not a diet I would recommend), which brought me back to my pre-menopausal weight, not underweight. It feels great to be back to normal weight-wise, with all my clothes fitting the way they should. Oddly, it wasn't the chemo that triggered my weight loss, it was my bout with a cold during the first phase of chemo. Go figure. My sinuses have stopped sloughing skin and seem to be healing. My finger numbness has stalled and doesn't seem to be getting any worse in terms of neuropathy. I never had symptoms in my feet that I can tell, so it's just my fingertips, and sometimes my lips feel a little tingly, but it's nothing too dramatic, just a new sensation to add to the list of firsts on this adventure.

Yes, it's an adventure, and like all adventures, sometimes the sun shines, and sometimes it rains. For the most part, so far this adventure has had sunny skies. Remember, this was a mandatory trip, sort of like taking a business trip to a city you have no desire to go to. Even if I didn't want to go, there has always been something to take away, to point to and say, "I wouldn't have missed that for the world." My experience bank so far has more I-wouldn't-miss-that-for-the-world moments than this-sucked-beyond-belief experiences, so I think I'm doing pretty darn well. This book is one of them, as are the comments of support and encouragement. Thank you all for reading, for sharing, for making sure this finds its way to others who might benefit from it so they too might find a reason to smile as they make their way on their own journey, whatever that may be. Oh, and please remind them to bring a flashlight. I have found that everything looks better in the light.

Chapter 27 - The Cancer Kraken

Have you ever had a day when everything seemed to go wrong? When despite your best efforts, you can't right your ship and it continues to take on water until it finally sinks, one long, drawn-out glub-glub at a time? Friday, February 24 was like that for me. I have gone over the day again and again, wondering if maybe it really wasn't the comedy of errors it seemed to be, if it was just my perspective of events and not the actual happenings that were awry, but I don't think so. I think I could have had a better attitude towards the end, and I tried, really I did, but sometimes the ship is meant to sink no matter what you do or think.

Friday, February 24 was my post-chemo follow-up MRI to determine the effect of the sixteen treatments on my breast cancer tumor. I left the house at 7:30 a.m. so I could be there by 8:30 a.m. for registration and 9 a.m. for my MRI appointment. I wasn't supposed to eat or drink for two hours before the appointment so I wanted to be in and out of there. Not eating didn't bother me, but my mouth still gets dry (a side effect of chemo that hasn't worn off yet), and so three hours is about my limit with no water, and that's when I'm asleep. During the day was bound to be a different story.

Traffic was uncharacteristically light, and I was at Orlando Health by 8 a.m. I got registered and settled in to wait for my appointment. Then, out of the blue, my ship had its first hole punched in it. I never saw it coming; it was the cancer kraken, I'm sure of it. All day, piece by piece, my ship called *Normal* was pulled apart, until I had no choice but to give in and let it sink, pulled into the deep by the tough-love arms of the cancer kraken. Here's what happened, glub by glub.

9 a.m. - The MRI nurse came to get me and then explained they don't access ports in imaging. If I wanted to use my port for the dye contrast, I would have to go over to the Ambulatory Care Center to have it accessed, which is in another building (I saw no

need to have my arm punctured when I had a perfectly good port). By the time I got there and back, she had taken another patient. (Glub)

10 a.m. - Still waiting. Keep in mind I had been up since 6:30 a.m. with no water except to rinse my mouth when I brushed my teeth. The nurse finally came and got me again as I was nicely asking the front desk person how much longer they thought it might be.

10:40 a.m. - MRI is done and I'm headed back to the Ambulatory Care Center to have them de-access my port. There was some confusion once I got there because they thought I should have had lab work done with the MRI (actually before the MRI). (Glub) I finally told them to just draw the labs and if they needed them, great, and if they didn't, throw them away. They drew the labs, de-accessed the port, and I was on my way.

11:30 a.m. - On the road and headed to work. I guzzled some amazingly delicious water in the car and ate the piece of cinnamon raisin toast I'd brought for breakfast.

A funny sidebar, although not so funny at the time, as I was driving back to the office, my port began to gurgle. I could feel it, in my chest, a gurgling. That has never happened, and my guess was it shouldn't ever happen (Glub-glub!)

12 p.m. - Got to the office and spent the next fifteen minutes calling my surgeon's office to find out if my port gurgling was a critical issue or if somehow the gals in MRI had broken it. The doctor said he doubted it was broken and more likely fluid had collected in a pocket around the port and it would be fine. I should call back if it showed any signs of infection. For the next two hours, every fifteen minutes or so my port would gurgle; sound effects for my sinking ship.

1 p.m. - I was barely at the office an hour when my cell phone rang. It was my oncologist's nurse. My potassium levels were

critically low and I had to go back to Orlando Health for a potassium infusion. They had an opening at 1:30 p.m. (Glub, glub)

1:20 p.m. - Back at Orlando Health, looking for food. All I've eaten all day is a piece of toast, and the infusion will be two hours. The cafe in the Heart Center (across from the Ambulatory Care Center) is cleaning up from lunch and has no avocado wraps, or wraps of any kind, left. Then, as I round the corner on my way to the Ambulatory Care Center, a valet rounded it full tilt from the other direction and almost ran into me, scaring the heck out of me. The gal behind me asked me if I was okay and I responded by asking her if she knew where I could find some food. She was kind enough to take me to the big cafeteria; it was overwhelming. Try as I might, I couldn't find any sort of pre-made salad or sandwich that didn't have soy something in it. (What's with the new obsession with putting soy in everything!) I aborted the food hunt and went to my infusion appointment. (Glub)

1:35 p.m. - I had my port accessed for a second time in one day—a first for this adventure—and was transferred to an infusion station and waited for my potassium order to come up.

2 p.m. - The nurse showed up with my potassium infusion, set it up, and left me to wait, sadly none too patiently. (Glub) All they had to eat in the infusion room was applesauce, fruit in syrup and Sun Chips; I declined. By my calculations, I'd be out of there by 4 p.m., beat rush hour, and be home in time for an early dinner. I should have learned by now, on this day of all days, not to plan.

2:30 p.m. - The nurse came back to check my drip. It seems she put the rate in too slow. My two-hour infusion has now grown to a three-hour infusion. I asked for a bag of Sun Chips, which, by the way, give you indigestion if eaten on an empty stomach. (Glub, glub, glub)

4 p.m. - The infusion nurse has gone home and I am back to the nurse who accessed my port. She started my second potassium drip. I'm in the home stretch!

5:15 p.m. - Bag two is done. Port is flushed, de-accessed and I'm ready to hit the road. Just in time for rush hour. (Glub)

There is eerily no traffic, again.

I tried all day not to get angry or frustrated, not at the MRI gals, not at Nurse Mary, not at the cafeteria for being too big to do anything on the fly and for using soy in their pre-packaged foods, but it was hard. With nothing to do but watch the drip of potassium and rehash the day, it was also hard not to pause as I imagined my battered ship slipping beneath the waves and realizing how easily the day's events had crippled it.

So what was it really, that day of the sinking ship? A training ground, or a test, and did I pass or fail? And if I failed, what was I even being tested on? Maybe it was just a reminder that I have cancer, and it doesn't go in a straight line, and sometimes you are going to be inconvenienced, and maybe it's all for the good. I have been lucky, I haven't really been inconvenienced by my cancer, other than the obvious, but maybe I need to be. Maybe I need to let myself be disrupted more often to remind me what is important and not slip back into old habits.

As of late, I've been gravitating back to that familiar space that I used to call normal, when in reality there is no normal for me anymore, there is only now, the space between what was once my normal and what will become my new normal in the future. It is a strange place, this no-man's land of half steps and unsure footing, but a necessary stop on my journey. It is the place where my old familiar ship called *Normal* sinks and makes way for a new boat to be built to take its place, one that can navigate the waters called breast cancer survivor, one that is strong and sturdy and won't take on water when inconvenienced. One that is a more worthy opponent for the cancer kraken.

SURGERY

Chapter 28 - The Magic of Meditation

I meditated a lot during my chemo treatments. I had important work to do, and meditating was a great way to get laser focused on my goals and how to accomplish them. When I meditate, I go deep inside myself, I find that place that connects me with the universe, and I listen. It's like being in a train station, only no one is going anywhere, not even me. I'm just people watching, eavesdropping on dozens of conversations at the same time, and all the conversations are wisps of thought intended for me.

If I listen really closely, I can hear them, feel them wash over me. They feel like puffs of love, warm breezes of sensation that my brain seems to have no trouble translating into words. Sometimes the sensations are just reassuring feelings, like peace, or calm, that wrap around me, usually in response to a problem or question I might have. Other times they are direct responses, so powerful they cannot be ignored or discounted. Regardless, I have learned that in the end, the answer to every question must begin with a state of peace or calm. I cannot tackle a problem in a state of agitation, nor can I pick out a more complicated message among the throng of conversations going on around me if they also have to compete with turmoil in my head. No, first, I must find a state of peace and calm, and then I can tackle the problem. And so it is with the next phase of my breast cancer adventure, the surgery phase.

I met with my oncologist, Dr. Regan Rostorfer, and surgeon, Dr. Jeffrey Smith, on February 28, 2017, and received the fantastic news that my breast cancer tumor had shrunk "markedly." It is literally a shadow of its original size when comparing the before and after MRIs. The original pre-chemo reading was 6 by 3 centimeters in size and it shrank to a post-chemo follow-up reading of 1.5 by .6 centimeters in size, and my lymph nodes show no detectible evidence of cancer either, which was my primary goal for the chemo treatments. Before chemo, a mastectomy was really my only surgery option. With a tumor size of 6 centimeters, a lumpectomy was just not feasible. Now, I am suddenly in a position of having surgery options. I'd like to say the decision was hard, that I agonized over it, but in reality it wasn't hard at all. When I meditate on decisions, or life choices, or whatever I am faced with really, if I find that place of peace and calm and begin my inquiries from there, things become clear. I have an easier time of wading through the clutter and getting to the real crux of the question. And so it was with my surgery decision.

The first thing I'm going to say is that this decision is the best decision for me and me alone. Everyone is different. We all have different situations, value the pros and cons that come with surgery and reconstruction options differently, and have a different relationship with ourselves physically, mentally, emotionally and spiritually. There are no right or wrong or good or bad decisions, there is only what is best for each of us based on our own personal situation. As part of my decision-making process, I asked question after question of my doctors, and when I was done I asked the doctors what questions I should be asking that I wasn't. I wanted to know everything. This is my body, my vessel, and I want to know the short-term and long-term effects of everything that would happen to it, to me, with every surgery and reconstruction option. I have done this throughout my entire treatment plan, with chemo, with radiation, and now with surgery and reconstruction.

I don't usually offer advice, but I will say this, Orlando Health encouraged me to meet with all the departments I might need services from (chemo, radiation, reconstruction, and surgery) before I began treatment. That way I had a team assembled and wasn't trying to find doctors and make decisions on the fly when I arrived at a point when I would need services. Cancer treatment travels a crooked path, and no matter how resolute your opinions are going in, they have a way of changing with the bends in the road. I found it very helpful to meet with each department, learn all I could about what the treatments entailed, the pros and cons, benefits and potential long-term physical damage. I also tried to get a sense of what I would be open to if faced with the need to have surgery, or reconstruction, or radiation, or chemotherapy. Feelings change, so it was advantageous to have time to let the information sink in before having to make a final decision on a treatment option. Had I needed to do it on the fly, my decisions and treatment outcomes may have been different. For instance, going into my diagnosis, I was adamantly against chemo, but when faced with the option of potentially losing lots of lymph nodes, which could affect my quality of life for the rest of my life, or having chemo that would suck in the short term, but likely kill any cancer cells in my lymph nodes and lessen the number that would potentially have to be removed during surgery, my stance changed. My feelings changed. I could still have declined chemo, as I can decline any treatment option, but I chose my own path for my own reasons, which is what matters. I was in control.

An important part of my cancer journey for me has been to not get ahead of myself. Once I was educated on all the potential aspects of treatment, I set it all aside. These sorts of life-changing procedures trigger gut reactions. I let those reactions have their say, then put them on a shelf until it was time to look at that stage of treatment again. For surgery and reconstruction, that time is now.

When you start with a large tumor, your surgery options are pretty limited. Mastectomy and/or a palliative double mastectomy. Now I was offered the option of having a mastectomy or trying a lumpectomy with the understanding that there was a chance I would need to come back for a mastectomy depending on the pathology. My husband and I had already spent weeks discussing this and I had spent just as much time meditating on it. As my chemo wound down, there was really no avoiding it. Once my follow-up MRI was scheduled, around week thirteen of my chemo, surgery fell off the shelf and demanded to be looked at, to be felt.

In the days I spent meditating on surgery, I'll be honest, I was looking for an answer, or a feeling that might guide me. I wanted someone else to tell me what to do. Crazy, right? I had spent months happily controlling my own destiny and now I wanted to defer. Well, meditation doesn't work that way. It was there, my mind adrift among the whispers of helpful souls, that I didn't get the answer I wanted, but the question I needed. Clear as a bell, the only important question was asked, not by me, but of me. The question was, *Which choice will accomplish your goal?*

For the entirety of my chemo treatment, I had asked the angels to please heal my body of cancer so that I could live a long, productive, cancer-free life. Given the question, the answer was obvious. On March 20, 2017, I am having a double mastectomy. I have also opted to forgo reconstruction. I believe the buzz phrase now is "going flat." It is a personal choice and one I am comfortable with based on what is important to me and my husband.

Am I afraid? Sometimes. Not of surgery or cancer, but of the personal strength I will need to proudly navigate the "flat" path I have chosen. I spent fifty-five years with breasts, my new silhouette will no doubt take some getting used to. And no, I don't think it would be any easier if I opted for reconstruction. I have never allowed societal norms to define my opinion of myself, and do not plan to start now. My body is a vessel, a home for my soul as it experiences the wonders of life. I don't think fake boobs are going to help on that front. The real ones never did.

Chapter 29 - Fear(less), Guilt(less), Breast(less)

Finally, tears. Tears of ... something, not sure what. Grief, Stage 2, so I'm told. Tears, loss of appetite, sleep disturbance ... check, check, and check.

I feel ... guilty. Not about cancer, or surgery, or tears, but about being so damn needy. Thank God for my husband, Ken. Without his hand to hold on to, I'm lost. Without his reassuring, steady voice to talk me out of the abyss, I'm lost. Without him, I am lost. See, needy. Really, really needy. Still, thank God for Ken. Without him, I am *lost*.

I'm not afraid of the surgery, I'm afraid of surgery. It's a general fear, not really specific to this surgery, just an overarching fear of the dead space you are in when under anesthesia. I don't remember that time when I wake up. It is lost, forever, a no-man's land of nothingness that is not forgotten, because there is nothing to remember. It just doesn't exist, for me. Where do I go? What do I think? Two hours is a long time to be nowhere thinking of nothing, or nowhere thinking of something that you can't remember, can't reclaim, ever. It can make you crazy if you dwell on it, and I have a week to dwell on it.

One week from today, I will be breast-less. That doesn't bother me, doesn't frighten me, doesn't faze me. I'm too busy getting there, counting down to the surgery, to my trip to no-man's land. Today, to commemorate the start of the final countdown, there were tears. A rain of glistening confetti to jump-start my final march toward debreastation (okay, not actually a word, but it has an appropriate ring to it).

I guess the good news in all this is I won't remember the actual surgery. We have progressed a lot since the days of taking a swig of whiskey and biting on a stick. Now, we simply lose time. We slip off to sleep then wake up thinking we just closed our eyes for a moment, then surprise! Surgery is done; snap out of it and you can go home. That happened to me when I went in for my port surgery. I thought I was languidly waiting with Ken in preop and I closed my eyes for a moment, just dozed off for a few seconds, and it was over. I was in post-op and had missed it, the signal that I was being sent off to nowhere and in short order would be back. It haunts me, that loss of time, of control, and all because I didn't get the signal.

So maybe that is the crux of the problem. At the root of it all is my control freak nature pissed off that they snuck up on me and put me under without even a "count to ten." Fifteen minutes under for port surgery is fine for that sort of tactic, but two hours and then no breasts? I need to mentally prepare for that, to take a deep breath, say one final goodbye to ... what? Physical appendages? Farewell dear mammary glands, it's been a good ride?

Even writing this it sounds ludicrous, but like it or not, we have a deep-seated attachment to the comfort of our appearance. And I, as okay as I am with this surgery, am now goaded by that very okay-ness. There has to be a reaction forthcoming, looming on the horizon, shrouded in a mist, of tears perhaps?

Hopefully this galleon of emotion will not materialize on Monday morning while I'm waiting for a shroud of nothingness to descend and hoping I don't miss the signal.

Chapter 30 - Bee Stings and Dinosaurs

Another glorious day in sunny Florida. I had a fabulous day, pre-planned to be exceptional since it is my last day of unfettered movement for the next ten days. Tomorrow is debreastation day, so what better way to go into surgery than with a happy heart and a smile on my face.

The delightful gals in nuclear medicine over at Orlando Health let me move my appointment from this afternoon to this morning, giving me the rest of the day to enjoy. First though, nuclear medicine. I know you are wondering, so I'll share. As part of the surgery, they are going to remove and biopsy what are called the sentinel lymph nodes. Put simply, these are the lymph nodes the tumor drains to first. To find them, the day before the surgery (today) I went in to have radioactive material injected into my breast. Then the day of the surgery (tomorrow), I go back to nuclear medicine and they will take pictures of the glowing lymph nodes.

Cool, right? Even cooler still, in the operating room they will use a sort of handheld Geiger counter to find the radioactive lymph nodes. Between the pictures and the Geiger counter, the rummaging around to find the nodes will be at a minimum. And, in case those two aren't enough to find the right ones, the injection had dye in it as well so the sentinel nodes will have turned blue. It's kind of hard to miss a radioactive blue lymph node, right?

Back to the injection. When I talked to the nuclear medicine tech on Friday, he may have oversimplified one thing about the procedure. It hurts like holy hell. It's a short time in hell, I will give it that, but it is a pain like no other. The appointment itself was quick and easy, just as he said. You go in, take off your shirt and bra, put on a gown and lie down on a bed. I sneaked a peak at the needle; it was tiny. Teeny, tiny. Bee sting tiny. When the needle slides under your skin, it really is no big deal. Then Mary (she was delightful, by the way), injects the material. It is a climbing pain, one that starts out simple and culminates in grab-the-side-of-the-bed agony. It doesn't sting, it doesn't burn, it is just pain. It was so painful I couldn't even swear. All I could come up with was, "Oh, my, GOD." Long, slow, oh ... my ... GOD! I was just about to beg Mary to stop, when it was over. She put a piece of gauze over the injection spot and rubbed it vigorously and it was gone. The pain vanished. It didn't dissipate, it was just gone. There is no appropriate response for the sudden alleviation of excruciating agony, so I laughed, and couldn't stop. I peppered it with commentary, making it even more funny, and Mary laughed with me.

At the time I likened the injection to a snake bite, which is what I imagined was an upgrade from a bee sting, but I've actually never been bitten by a snake, so I really don't have any frame of reference. The tech I spoke to on Friday said the injection is "not comfortable." I thought it strange at the time, I mean why not say "uncomfortable"? Why say "not comfortable"? Because uncomfortable is too soft sell. Plain and simple, it's really not comfortable. Plus, I think if they tell patients it is excruciating agony the likes of which you have never felt before, but it doesn't last long, they may get a lot of no-shows. Stick with not comfortable; they can always hold on to the bed.

With that out of the way, Ken and I spent the day at Leu Gardens in Orlando. The gardens are fabulous, with a wide variety of plants and trees that are all well marked in case you want to try your luck at home. They have a dinosaur exhibit going on through the end of April, which I didn't want to miss. It's very well done, with life-size dinosaurs staged throughout the gardens amid the foliage. I'm ashamed to say we have lived in the Orlando area for over ten years and this is the first time we have been to Leu Gardens. It was wonderful, but for a quieter experience next time we will try the middle of the week. There were lots of very excited young children, but in hindsight, what did we expect, there are dinosaurs there!

So, having spent a perfect day outside with the dinosaurs amid the foliage with the love of my life, how could it get any better? I'm home, cooking. Nothing says surgery-is-no-big-deal like baking bread and cooking soup. I'm not a fan of chicken noodle soup, but it is Ken's favorite, so there's a big pot simmering on the stove. It will make for easy meals when I'm not in a cooking mood post-surgery.

Since today is my last day with breasts, I suppose I should share my thoughts on it. They are pretty breasts, and I'm sure the left one will look quite spectacular lit up with radioactive Christmas lighting, but I am not quite over the fact that it tried to kill me. Not entirely its fault, I suppose, but it has resulted in, shall we say, an enormous amount of inconvenience and pain on my part, the most recent being this morning, so again, I'm not over it. To that end, and for probably a whole host of other conscious and subconscious reasons, I currently feel nothing. No sense of loss, no sense of misgiving, no sense of woe is me. Nothing, nada, zip.

There is, of course, always tomorrow. I have imagined myself partially sedated attempting to have some sort of half-baked discussion on my change of heart or plans or both as they wheeled me into surgery, but it was a fleeting thought and didn't stick. I don't see a healthy future for me with breasts, so I am soldiering on without them.

I've had time to get used to it, to wrap my head around things. I've scoured the Internet for photos so I know what to expect visually. They are largely ornamental at my age, and as anyone over fifty can attest, the ornaments don't get better the older they get. They take a lot more work to maintain and tend to gravitate toward the lower branches of the tree, if you get my drift. So, while I would never go into this voluntarily, since the situation has presented itself, I will do what I do best, I will make the most of it.

I see no downside to not having breasts. A change in my breast size will not change me as a woman or as a person. What goes on in my head is, as always, good thoughts, happy thoughts, imaginings of endless possibilities.

What goes on in your head?

Chapter 31 - The Art of a Happy Surgery

Monday, March, 20, was surgery day. Everything turned out better than great. It turned out awesomely fantastically great! They took three lymph nodes and they all tested negative for cancer, which was my primary concern. Still loving the remodel. There are no bandages over the surgery sites, just steri-strips, so I was able to peek down at them, or lack of them, depending on your viewpoint, and I liked what I saw. It looked natural, oddly enough, so no regrets, none whatsoever. All and all, I'm in a pretty amazing place, which is a pretty special place to be in the days after a double mastectomy.

The path to amazing land was not easy, though, because the path to surgery la-la land was not easy. You will appreciate it, I think, and hopefully laugh along with me, because it really was funny as hell. It's a tad long, but hang in there. The ending rocks!

6:00 a.m. - We arrived at Orlando Health, more than on time for my 7 a.m.. appointment with imaging in nuclear medicine. I checked in at patient registration and then waited. And waited. And waited. There was an amusing older guy in the waiting room with buzzed white hair, a toothless jowly face, and overalls. He had a drawl of sorts and his jabbering at the front-desk lady across the room, mostly about the temperature in the waiting room, kept me amused. He was with a middle-aged woman with an oxygen tank who never seemed quite satisfied with her wheelchair. At one point she left and came back with another one. The process to transfer all her belongings from one chair to another took several people—her, another woman who was with her, and finally Ken when he saw her struggling with a large bag she was trying to hang on one of the high poles at the back of the chair.

Eventually 7 a.m. came and went without my name being called, so I went to the registration desk and inquired as to whether I should find my own way to nuclear medicine. Usually a volunteer takes patients to the different departments from registration. It prevents patients from getting lost in the maze of halls. A volunteer who had been sitting waiting for a route jumped on the opportunity and took Ken and I and another patient up to nuclear medicine. The day had now officially begun.

7:15 a.m. - It takes a while to get through the maze of hallways. Thank goodness for the volunteers whose job it is to walk patients to their treatment areas! In another ten minutes I was taken back to the photography area for my close-up. You don't need to take anything off (unless you are wearing anything radioactive). You just lie on your back fully clothed, arms over your head, and relax. The camera is silent, so a nap is doable, but if you don't like MRIs, you will hate this. The camera is about 4 feet by 4 feet (I'm guessing, it seemed really big), and when it slides over you it covers your torso and head. Then it lowers down and comes to a stop about 6 inches above you.

I like to peek in MRIs. If I can crawl out, I'm good, I don't feel trapped. This one would have been tough, but with some wiggling and wriggling I could have slid out sideways, so was okay with it, although I did peek from time to time to make sure the camera didn't get any lower.

8:00 a.m. - After nuclear medicine, a transportation associate (fancy name for a staff member who walks you to your next appointment) walked us over to breast care imaging. Us means Ken, my husband, and I. My fabulous husband has been with me every step of the way through my breast cancer treatment, and surgery day was no different. The next appointment was the one I had been dreading. Way back in the annals of my breast cancer adventure, during the testing phase, I had a lymph node biopsy. That node was going to be removed during surgery. So the surgeon could find it, they were sticking a guide wire into it. I have never had a good experience with biopsies, so I couldn't imagine sticking a wire into my lymph node would be any better. Waiting to have someone stick a wire into your lymph node definitely makes it worse.

8:45 a.m. - After holding on to Ken's hand for forty-five minutes, resting my head on his shoulder, and in general doing anything and everything I could to keep my shit together, I went back to the women's imaging area. Ken wasn't allowed back there; it is women only. A nurse took my paperwork and I settled into the waiting room. The front-desk woman had me change into a gown and put my clothes in a bag, my signal that I wouldn't be wearing them again anytime soon. (How's that for getting real fast?)

9:15 a.m. - The technician came to get me and took me into what looked like a mammogram torture room. I asked her exactly how this procedure was going to happen, since I was here just to get a wire in a lymph node. She looked puzzled and asked me what surgery I was having. When I said a double mastectomy, she said she would be right back, she needed to talk to the doctor. I waited another half an hour before she came back and said I was in the wrong room and would be transferred to a sonar imaging room. They were prepping the room for me.

10 a.m. - I was transferred to sonar imaging, which was like old home week, but not in a warm, fuzzy reunion kind of way. The people were great, but I did have a lymph node biopsy last time I was here and I was going to have a wire stabbed into the very same lymph node, so happy-to-be-here wasn't my top emotion. The imaging technician took an image of my armpit and then the doctor came in. Same doctor as before, Doctor Gross. He's a nice guy, great at explaining everything he is going to do and thankfully great at sticking to his plan. Still, I don't have a lot of flesh, so anywhere they stick a needle in my upper body hurts like hell, and this did too. Thankfully, the procedure was quick, but now it was bumping up on 10:30 a.m. and I had a date with a surgeon in an hour, so my anxiety level was starting to rise.

10:30 a.m. - They collected Ken, stuck me in a wheelchair, and we headed off to surgery. Waiting for the elevator, I cried. Not because I had a wire stuck in my underarm, not because I was having my breasts removed, but because I was running out of time. I had envisioned getting to pre-op an hour ago. I had envisioned having plenty of time to get settled, relax, spend time with Ken, and go off to surgery in a happy place, not a flurry of activity. So I cried. And I broke Ken's heart. This has all been such a strain on him, and he has been my rock, but this was too much. I told him I was fine, that I had just hoped to spend time with him before the surgery and now it was too late. I hoped it helped, made him feel a little better, but rocks don't really talk, so I can only hope.

10:35 a.m. - We are in pre-op and they sent Ken to the waiting room, and while I am signing off on paperwork, I start to cry again. The nurse was amazing. I explained to her that I was fine with the surgery, but it was so late and I wouldn't be able to spend time with my husband before surgery and that made me really sad. Her response—we'll go get him! And they did. Another nurse came to help with the pre-op and told Ken he would have to leave and my nurse said no, he can stay, and that was that. He stayed with me through the entire prep, and thank God he did or I probably wouldn't have handled it as well as I did. Here's the pre-op protocol at Orlando Health -

- they sent me to the bathroom to swab the inside of my nostrils with iodine and brush my teeth, swab my cheeks and gargle with antiseptic mouth rinse;

- back at my bed, they gave me antiseptic cleaning wipes, one for each arm, leg, my front and my back. I scrubbed myself, put on my gown and got into bed;

- on go the support hose and the leg massagers (my favorite), then they covered me with a warm blanket. Somewhere in all this they have taken my temperature and blood pressure.

Next comes the IV line and the fun began. Keep in mind I have not had anything to drink since 11 pm the night before (no eating or drinking after midnight the day before surgery). My veins are dried-up creek beds. (Tidbit—drink lots of water before you go to have blood work done and your veins will stand out better.) My nurse found a vein, gave me a little lidocaine, because the IV needle is BIG, and got the IV in fine. The flow stunk. There was a valve up-arm from where she put the needle in and it was making the flow inadequate, so she took the IV out and went for another spot closer to my hand. More lidocaine, needle goes in fine, flow is good. We have a winner.

NOT! In short order I feel pressure where she had put the first line in, and a large pool of blue is forming under my skin around the site. Apparently the new IV location is in the same vein just farther up the line and the pressure is causing the first site to leak. So that IV comes out.

Another nurse comes by to check on us because I'm supposed to be IV-ed by now and ready to go to surgery. The operating room is ready, so when I'm ready, they are ready. Pretty soon I have four nurses gathered around my bed discussing IV sites. I nix the inside of my elbow. The vein there sits right on top of my ligament, and hitting that ligament means a month of pain (personal experience). My nurse agreed. She could feel the ligament right under the vein. There was lengthy discussion about using a vein on the top of my hand, but there was no way to tell which vein fed the vein from the first two tries, so they decided to give the underside of my forearm a try.

By this time the assistant anesthesiologist has entered the mix and is chatting with me about what a good attitude I have. (I started laughing after the second IV try failed. I have always found humor to be the best medicine.) He bore a strong resemblance to the main actor from the TV show *Royal Pains*. It's funny, really— my doctor resembles an actor playing a doctor in a TV show. I told him and he looked it up on his phone. I can't believe no one has ever told him that before, since the nurses knew exactly what I was talking about.

I am starting to look like a war hero with all the gauze pads taped firmly on my IV wounds. Another nurse is giving the underside of my forearm a go, but in seconds a large swelling started so she took it out and started pressure on that site (I think she missed the vein, because the swelling looked like fluid, not blood). They start talking about accessing a deeper vein and call around for imaging equipment and the nurse who is good at accessing a deeper vein (everyone has their vein specialty apparently), when the anesthesiologist appears on the scene wondering where the heck his patient is. He parts the sea of nurses, sees my arm and declares he is going to do the IV himself. He declines their IV materials and calls for his own, sending nurses scurrying. Picasso was at work and he needed his own tools. He thumps around on my hand, tries my hand and decides that no vein is going to work, I'm too dehydrated. He asks me if I have a port, which I do. He said to access my port, start fluids, and bring me to the operating room. They will get started and once my veins are hydrated and plumped he will swap out the port line for an IV line. Then, like God having spoken, he left, and the nurses set to work.

By this time, I have been there so long, I have to go to the bathroom again. They unhook everything and send me to the bathroom. When I get back, they hook everything back up, access my port, and start fluids and some relaxants. I kissed Ken one last time and they wheeled me off to the operating room. And I remember it! Being wheeled in and seeing the classic operating-room lights overhead. They asked me to slide myself over to the operating table (they are amazingly narrow, which makes sense from a reach point of view), then the assistant anesthesiologist placed the oxygen mask over my face (I could tell it was him from his voice) and I wafted off to somewhere safe, because I felt safe.

It was funny how familiar the operating room looked, just like it does in every medical show you see on TV or in a movie. It was funny how peaceful it all felt. I trusted these people, which is not something I do easily. The anesthesiologist, who had proven himself already with his wisdom and calm in calamity, his assistant with his ready smile and calming demeanor, and my surgeon, Dr. Jeffrey Smith, who is one in a million. I was in good hands, I had volumes of prayers being said for me by friends and family, the Archangel Gabriel and his cohorts were sitting on shoulders and guiding hands, and I had an amazing man who loved me unconditionally waiting for me when I awoke.

It's funny, isn't it, that the most important part of the story is this last paragraph. The rest is pure entertainment ...

Chapter 32 – Laissez-Faire Post-Mastectomy Days

The days are flying by. I thought they would drag, being that I resemble a cyborg and am schlepping drain bulbs, but the drains are not nearly as annoying as they were made out to be. Maybe it is my laissez-faire attitude toward them (or everything). They do their thing, I do mine. I have them clipped to lanyards—one for each— and then the lanyards fastened to my shirt with a small binder clip to keep them from swinging around, so I hardly notice they are there. A tank top (it has to be a really stretchy one, because you have to get into it feet first) and a pair of lounge pants complete my fashion ensemble. I am dressed for comfort, and I have nailed it.

I have been pain free the entire week. The doctor gave me a nerve block injection, which feels like it is wearing off right on schedule. The feeling at the surgery site has gone from nothing, meaning absolutely nothing, to a strange sensation of healing. I can actually feel things knitting on the inside. It's hard not to imagine an infinitesimal construction crew with teeny tiny hard hats toiling away. It's painless, this microscopic repair process, so I just let my mini construction crew do their thing while I do mine (again with the laissez-faire attitude).

Ken did take me back to the doctor on Tuesday, because one of my drain bulbs was defective. They are called Jackson-Pratt drains. The concept is that you squeeze the bulb and put the stopper in and it causes suction on the drain line, which causes the excess fluid around the surgery site to drain out. The defective bulb was drawing air in from the outside so there was no suction on the drain line; it was actually preventing fluid from draining into the bulb. The line would fill up and that would be that. I spent the first night stripping the line of fluid when I woke up every couple of hours to drink water and pee (I was back in dry-mouth mode for the first couple of days). Maggie, Dr. Smith's nurse, replaced the bulb and all was fine after that. The doctor did say I looked amazing for having had a double mastectomy less than twenty-four hours prior, so that made me feel good. I come from hardy stock and it is serving me well.

Ken has been amazing through all this. He helps me navigate the drain tubes while getting in and out of my clothes, watches to make sure I do my post-mastectomy exercises twice a day, empties my drain bulbs twice a day and keeps a daily log of the amount of fluid in the bulbs and my temperature (Jackson-Pratt protocol), and makes sure I have healthy, healing meals. I have no doubt that angels really do walk among us, and I have one that lays his head next to mine at night to boot.

I do want to thank everyone who has called, texted, emailed and sent flowers, teddy bears, and fruit. You are all awesome! The energy of the universe is a powerful thing, and when enough people send positive vibes, prayers, and healing energy in one direction (in this case mine) it does powerful work. Never underestimate the power of the collective conscious. When we all focus our thoughts on the power of good, no matter what it is, then good will prevail, or in my case, healing.

I do want to warn anyone I called on Monday night, I don't remember a thing. Hopefully my post-anesthesia dialing was all positive and happy. It seems to have been, as I was feeling pretty good. I was glad to be in my own bed and not a hospital bed, so kudos to Dr. Smith for letting that happen and not keeping me overnight at the hospital. The cat has figured out how to cuddle with me without interfering with the tubes and bulbs, and her familiar purr helps me sleep. With her on one side and Ken on the other, I am blessed to sleep in a love sandwich every night. It really doesn't get much better than that.

Chapter 33 - Baffled and Fascinated ... by a Drain

I'm both baffled and fascinated by my drains. They should annoy me, but it's not every day you have an opportunity to watch excess body fluid get gently sucked out of your body by a plastic bulb, so instead I choose to be intrigued.

One would think healing would go in a straight line. I thought it would start at Point A and progress to another letter in the alphabet. Not so, my friend, not so. It is a complex fickle process that only God, surgeons, and surgeons' assistants understand, and which I now get to watch from the front row.

Not all drains are alike, nor are all mastectomy sites. For me, the left side is the more productive side. It drains like a champion, siphoning copious amounts of velvet red fluid. The right side, on the other hand, has always been somewhat of a slacker. I would like to blame the defective bulb at the start, which was, after all, on the right, but the blame would be misplaced. My right side is simply uninterested, preferring to trickle a steady dribble of golden nectar rather than compete with its torso mate in any fashion.

And so it has been for eight days. Imagine my surprise when yesterday, one week and change after debreastation day, the tables turned and the right side ran red and the left side golden. The color change on the left side was not without fanfare (the left side is proving to be quite the showman). It all started when Ken suggested we strip the lines, a politically correct way of saying we should squeeze all the fluid from the tubes and down into the bulbs. Imagine my surprise when long, stringy threads of red clotted yuck snaked through the left line and into the bulb, followed by a river of golden nectar (I'm thinking the golden color is the better color, as not bleeding is always better than bleeding, be it internally or externally). The right side showed no interest in our efforts and continued its usual uneventful dribbling. The left side, on the other hand, engaged with gusto and finished with a finale of leaking through the bandage around the tube hole in my side and soaking my tank top. Bravissimo!

There is also no rhyme or reason as to how much drains out. Being logical in nature, I imagined it would drain effusively at the start, what I call Point A, and taper off, draining less and less, until it arrived at, let's say, a meager piddle at Point D. That gave me Points B and C to navigate before sticking the finish. Little did I know it would act more like a tennis or ping pong match than a road trip, with Point A being the serve and Points B and C being what I now see is the ten-day volley before (hopefully) accomplishing game, set and match point.

Even the rate of play varies. The right side is a steady, albeit boring, player, holding at 10 to 20cc every twelve hours, and the left side is all over the court, ranging from 20cc to as much as 50cc every twelve hours. Entertaining, maybe; illogical, definitely. If fables hold true and slow and steady does indeed win the race, then my money is on the right side.

So why the obsession with these drains? Well, they are hanging around my neck and are hard to miss, but not even I believe that. The truth is, unless the left side stops its shenanigans and slows down to 25cc per day, I'm going to be stuck with these drains for some time to come. Four days at 25cc per day is the benchmark for removal, a mark that has been within my reach several times, until lefty pulled one of her usual stunts. I'm hoping that after yesterday's pièce de résistance, lefty will be satisfied to leave the stage for a bit and follow the softer tempo of her torso mate. Slow and steady will, after all, win this race.

Chapter 34 - Happiness Is a State of Mind

Happiness is a state of mind, yet few of us choose to dwell there permanently. I find that, like everywhere I've lived, I get bored and end up taking jaunts elsewhere, sort of mini vacations, to places like Angerville, Frustration City, or Sad Town. Not often, mind you, as they are never as advertised and, quite honestly, the weather is never great in any of those places, but I'd be lying if I didn't admit to testing the waters again (and again) now and then.

What makes us revisit these undesirable vacation spots even after poor experiences the first time around? I suspect we need them, these weekends away in locales like Crap Town, to appreciate what we have. Where I live, the sun is pretty much always shining (literally and figuratively). I don't often find things to stew over, except maybe not having enough time to enjoy the perpetual good weather. It is of my own choosing, though, and I can change that, should change that, although admittedly probably won't change that (it's a work in progress). I don't really get angry, but I do get frustrated, which can look like anger even though it's more of a frustration-anger hybrid. (Let's dub it "frangry.") I am logic based and like to reason my way through things, navigating facts like stars to find my way through the dark. Well, newsflash, cancer is illogical, and the path to health cannot be charted. (Insert "frangry" here!) It is guesswork, hope and prayer, and laughter, lots of laughter.

So here is the skinny ... we all have cancer cells growing in us all the time. Yup, as unpopular as that is, it is the truth. Our cells are constantly going awry and our immune system is constantly cleaning them up and keeping the "unwanted" population to a minimum, until it doesn't. Then, like me, and millions of others, we end up with discernible cancer, a bland way of saying my population of cancer cells has reached critical mass in one locale and is large enough to be detected through diagnostic procedures.

Then there are the diagnostic procedures—sonar imaging, mammograms, biopsies, MRIs, CT scans, PET scans, and on and on and on. Just like the rides at Disney, Universal Studios, and Six Flags, diagnostic tests have a size limit too. If the cancer cluster is too small, it doesn't see it. If you think on it too hard, you end up with a one-way ticket to Funk Town. I don't think on it; I prefer to reason my way through it.

Reason, it's an odd thing humans do, analyzing the crud out of something that frightens us that we don't have a clue about until we have boxed and bowed it and made it presentable to ourselves and others. Being a tad different, and a tad indifferent, I go through the reasoning process in an entirely different fashion. Instead of analyzing the crud out of it, say cancer for instance, I analyze the crud.

There are some things that are very comforting about the ever-present aspect of cancer, and some things that are truly terrifying. If the body is designed to clean up the miscreant buggers, great! I can, in theory, just let it do its thing and move on. Oh, wait, it failed miserably. Okay, maybe not miserably, but it did fail. I do, after all, have breast cancer, which means my immune system did not keep said cells in check and they went, well, crazy. It was an epic cancer party, I am imagining, which landed me where I am, breaking up the festivities and cleaning up the debris. Which begs the question, will it happen again?

It could. And then again, maybe it won't. It is here, folks, we have to sprinkle logic liberally with faith, hope, and prayers. It doesn't do me, or you, or anyone, any good to take this opportunity to take up residence of any length in Angerville, Frustration City, Sad Town or Funk Town. If you must go, I recommend an overnight stay, two nights tops, and then home with you to more pleasant surroundings.

Anger, frustration, sadness, even the occasional funk, can be therapeutic and healing, but spend too much time there and you are simply wasting time. Life isn't great in those cities. In reality, it sucks in them. So visit, dabble, sample the lousy cuisine, dreary architecture and unsmiling populace, then go home and revel in the joy that is your life. There is, after all, no place like home.

Chapter 35 - Flat Blue Sky

I was lying in the hammock last weekend wondering what happened. The chemo portion of my breast cancer treatment was so full of optimism, bravery, joy even, and now everything is just plain flat. I turned to the sky hoping for an amusing cloud shape to brighten my mood, but there was nothing. It was a dull, flat blue, to match my dull, flat blue mood.

Jill, our cat, has become enamored with the hammock. She stretches out across it, easily taking up the second-man side, and doesn't want to be bothered by anyone or anything. The gentle sway lulls her into a place I remember all too well, but lately eludes me. One difference, I wasn't cranky about it. Jill treats the hammock like her Precious, and anyone that interferes or tries to part her from it immediately is recast as the enemy. I, personally, enjoy her company on the hammock and am delighted at her newfound obsession, however baffling it may be.

Jill doesn't sit on furniture as a rule, or on laps. She prefers solid ground beneath her paws. That is, until she discovered the hammock. Or maybe, in her intuitive sagacity, she was merely trying to tempt me back to a place where I find peace. Funny thing, after I ensconced myself on the hammock on Saturday, she sat with me for a while then abandoned it for a sunny spot on top of the patio table. Rolling over now and then to catch a glimpse of me from the corner of her eye, she casually watched me watching her.

And there it was, my bright spot peeking out, at long last! Watching her enjoy her perch in the sun, her sides rising and falling in deep, rhythmic purrs, I could feel a spark of joy ignite and begin to grow. I only need to fan the ember, to coax it to a flame.

It's been a while since I've written. I find it hard to write about flat things. Regardless, flat or not, they may help someone in their (breast) cancer journey or in their generic health journey, so here goes:

- **Drains** - One drain came out ten days after surgery and the second one after seventeen days. No, you cannot feel it when they pull the drain out. If anything, it feels like a little pressure and then it is over. There are plenty of YouTube videos out there of drains being removed. Watch one if you have a drain removal in your future and you will feel more relaxed going into it. I did.

After the second drain was removed, I ended up with a small hematoma where the drain tube sat under the scar. After seventeen days, my body was over it and ready to be rid of the drain. It was different from the fluid that collected on the right side, which is soft and normal colored (a seroma). The hematoma turned dark red and almost started to look like a bruise. I smeared Mayan Clay (yep, straight from the Yucatan!) on it and it went away in a couple of days. Mayan Clay pulls out impurities and soothes the skin. I've used it for insect bites and sunburn with amazing results. It takes out the burn and the itch. It's my go-to cure all for skin irritations and toxic reactions.

- **Cording** - Once the drains were out, I could start working on getting my movement back for real. The right side is fine. The extra week of limited activity on the left side seems to have been too long a time for taking it easy. Long story short, I have developed what is called "cording" in my left arm. Apparently there is no definitive reason as to what causes cording, but it is likely the lymphatic channel that was severed getting backed up and reacting. The result, a painful, tight spot on the inside of my left bicep just below my armpit. If you feel a strange pain in your arm around three weeks after lymph node surgery, get thee to a lymphatic therapy specialist, pronto!

I called over to the physical therapy center immediately and they got me in the next day, which was this morning. After an hour of painful stretching and massage, I found I had a very deep well to draw from for feeling sorry for myself. I have a high tolerance for certain kinds of pain—tooth pain, muscle pain, emotional pain—but not nerve pain. My cording seems to possibly involve the nerve, so when it stretches it twangs the nerve and creates an electric shock sensation. Do that long enough and, well, you've heard the term "gunning for bear." Apparently cording is a process and takes some time to work itself out, so I likely have a couple of months of "bear season." I do apologize in advance to anyone and everyone who ends up in the woods with me. I suggest you run ...

- **Erogenous scars** - I'm not really sure how to say this next piece, but I think it's important so I'm just going to spit it out—my scars are now six-inch-long nipples. Yep, that's right, the nerve endings are reattaching themselves and my scars have taken over where my nipples left off as erogenous zones, only times one thousand. If you, or someone you know, is considering mastectomy surgery and whether or not to do reconstruction, this is definitely something to consider. I went flat with no reconstruction, but have complete feeling back in the skin of my chest as well as the ability for tactile arousal through the breast area. With reconstruction, that is not possible. Your breasts will be dead. Of course, there is no guarantee that you will have the same experience I have, but I am not the only one. It's something to consider, a question to ask. No one told me this was a possibility and I never considered asking. Who knew the body was so adaptive!

- **My hair is growing back** - I developed a five o'clock shadow on my head right after surgery and it has now grown out to G.I. Jane length. It's fuzzy in places, hairlike in others, with some overzealous strands sticking out like alfalfa wisps here and there. I'm looking forward to my first haircut. I'm also taking suggestions for an I've-got-hair celebratory crazy color event where I dye my hair just because. It has to grow for another couple of weeks, so I have time to find that perfect out-of-this-world look, or color.

Thanks again for all your support and encouragement. A special shout-out to Mark Cooper for nudging me back into writing mode. When we connect with the universe, everything we need is always right around us. We need only open ourselves up and let it all in.

Chapter 36 - Cattle Prods and String Cheese

Throughout my breast cancer adventure, I have been asked the question, "Are you in pain?" My answer, until now, has always been a resounding "no." My cancer was not painful, although I will give a nod to some of the less pleasant diagnostic tests. My chemo was not painful, although I will give a nod to some of the less pleasant side effects. My double mastectomy surgery was not painful, although I will give a *vigorous* nod to the nuclear medicine injection the day before surgery, which still holds the honor of being the most painful thing I have *ever* experienced. So now, on the one-month anniversary of my debreastation surgery, I will fess up. I have met pain, and its name is Cording.

Before I send anyone into a tail spin, pain is relative and comes in many, many flavors. There is short pain that comes from, say, being stuck by a needle, the proverbial "bee sting," and chronic pain, like from arthritis or a wonky back, and then there is insidious pain that sneaks up on you and behaves in unnatural ways for no apparent reason and with no forewarning, hijacking parts of your body to torture you with, and providing no clear way to combat it.

But I digress. Cording pain only happens if I raise my arm higher than my shoulder. It's not shoulder pain, it's pain from an interloper. It seems a gremlin has taken up residence and stretched a cord (hence the name—cording) from the tip of my mastectomy scar down into my arm. He has appropriated what was once a lymph channel and now, being detached from its companion lymph node during surgery, he is using it for his own amusement, mainly my agony.

I'm not exactly sure when cording moved in. Since the drain stayed in for an extra week on the left side, I didn't try lifting my arm over my head for a good three weeks after surgery (doctor's orders, don't lift your arm higher than your shoulder until the drain comes out), and when I did ... YOWZA! It felt like someone had poked my bicep with a low-volt cattle prod (low volt for a cow, not for me!) My cording pain takes the form of an intense, sudden sensory overload, like an electric shock and nails on a chalkboard all wrapped up in the sensation that the guts of your arm are all stuck together, but trying to pull apart, with a nerve tangled up in the middle for good measure. Oh, and just for fun, the same motion never results in the same pain response, and some motions that were pain free yesterday result in agony today. And this can go on for up to two months, or maybe longer, or maybe forever, or so I'm told.

My patience went south fast with these shenanigans. Yes, shenanigans. I am the captain of my body and no disenfranchised lymph channel is going to hijack what would otherwise be a perfectly pleasant post-mastectomy pre-radiation break. If the cording gremlin wants to make me miserable, well, two can play at that game. I borrowed from all my physical training and yoga techniques to create my own fast-track cording rehab program to encourage the process along at a more realistic pace. One week later, my arm goes over my head without a whimper and I can move about freely without fear of the cattle prod. I still have moments, but they are ones I seek out to work on a touchy spot, not ones that sneak up on me.

Now keep in mind, everyone is different. We all meet cording in different ways and shoo him out in different ways again, but if any of this resonates with you, give it a try. With cording, I have found that the overwhelming advice is "try it." If it works, keep it; if not, then try something else. I would recommend clearing anything you want to test out with your doctor or occupational/physical therapist first, just to be sure it's right for you. Otherwise, here is my insane cording gremlin beater program:

- **Yoga** - Since the primary objective is to stretch the cord, yoga makes perfect sense. Rather than lie on my back and passively grit my teeth through a static stretch (been there, done that!), I went straight for Downward Facing Dog. I start off in Plank position (arms straight, think top of a pushup) then slowly rocked my hips back and up until the cord starts to complain. The first time I did this, the inside of my upper arm felt like string cheese being pulled apart. It hurt, but it also felt kind of cool. In Downward Facing Dog you can hang on the edge of ouch without moving into insane agony, and just let your body work itself out. When you have had enough, rock back to Plank. I take a break in Child's Pose, then back to Plank and Downward Facing Dog. It's never the same experience twice, so just hang on and enjoy the ride. If it sucks one time, it will likely feel different the next time.

- **Vibe plate** - If you want to up the ante, which of course, I always do, then Downward Facing Dog on a vibe plate is just the ticket. Turn on the plate, then same as above, start out in Plank pose with your hands on the plate and your feet on the ground. Rock the hips up and back and ease back toward Downward Facing Dog. You will notice I use the words "ease" and "toward." This is not intended to be a picture-perfect Downward Facing Dog, this is intended to chase a wee gremlin out of your arm, so keep your eye on the prize and focus. **Please do all these motions slowly and mindfully.** The vibe plate vibrates your arms as you work the poses, so the pain can't grab hold. The first time I did this, I could feel things ungluing inside my arm, without the agony of slow stretching. My gremlin is not a fan of the vibe plate, which is reason enough for me to spend time on it. I could almost picture him bouncing around in there, snatching at surfaces and being knocked loose as soon as it thought he had a fingerhold. Boo-ya! Take that, little squatter!

- **More yoga** - Stretch, stretch, stretch and twist, twist, twist. I stretch my chest lying over something. I started with a folded blanket and then moved to a yoga block and now a bolster. Siting on the floor with knees bent, lie back over your prop of choice so it is under your shoulders, using a second block or blanket under your head so you are comfortable. Then straighten your legs, put your elbows on the ground perpendicular to your torso so you make a T with your arms, then slowly lower your forearm to the ground, palms facing up. If this gets your gremlin's knickers in a twist, then put your forearm on a blanket and work your way to flat. Once this is mastered, raise the height of what you are lying on or increase the angle of your arms away from your sides. You can also rotate your arms so your palms face down and see how that feels. Play with it, have fun, find where the gremlin hides! Twisting is also great for pulling apart the scar tissue around the mastectomy scars. You can do seated twists or lying twists. When you feel your scar pull, then you are in the right place.

Massage - Massaging my arm didn't work for me. It just made it more sore. If it works for you, then do it! What does work for me is massaging the scar where the cord starts from and massaging my drain hole scar on that side. The surgery scar is the visible scar. There is a lot of internal scar tissue forming under my arm and around the drain hole that is contributing to the cording, so massaging that helps a lot. (I use Palmer's Intensive Solid Formula twice a day on them).

So that's cording, cattle prods, and string cheese and all. He is a gremlin, and he won't be staying long ...

RADIATION

Chapter 37 - A Tango with Breast Cancer

The devil may care, but I don't. Really, I don't. Having spent over fifty years trying to meet an insanely high bar of accomplishment for myself and feeling skewered when I couldn't meet it, I have hung up my track shoes and no longer engage in high jumping, pole vaulting, or any other sport that requires me to jump higher than is humanly possible. I am, for now, content to simply be me, flaws and all. And hopefully, since I am no longer expecting the incomprehensible from myself, I will also stop expecting it from others. No worries, I'm not going to go all sloppy-silly on you, I'm just dialing it down to make room for other things, like life.

Yes, life. Life is the thing that quietly slips by when you are so busy living that you don't have time to realize that you aren't really living at all. It's a sad state of affairs when you begin to wonder whether, up until now, you have gotten it wrong, focused on the wrong things. A tango with breast cancer will do that for you. It shakes up your reality, paints the humdrum in technicolor. It intensifies your everyday experiences, emotionally, physically, and spiritually. On the other hand, maybe it's normal to question anything and everything that tries to mess with your current reality, the current state of sappy happy that dogs my every step. Yes, there you have it, I'm happy, exceptionally extraordinarily happy.

From where I sit, life is indeed pretty darn great. It always is, if we let it. All we have to do is accept that anything and everything is a sip from the fountain of bliss and drink it all in with equal appreciation. I have come to enjoy the wide variety of everyday experiences around me, to trust that the unfolding day will bring a smorgasbord my way from which happiness will arise. Nothing is a bad experience, because every experience can make way for something meaningful and uplifting.

For instance, yesterday we had tickets to see Sheryl Crow in concert. By the time the afternoon rolled around, I was feeling tired and knew that if I went to the concert I would be exhausted for days to come (cancer 101—don't overdo it!). Ken, my husband, and I bantered back and forth about going or not going and finally settled on giving the tickets away. A nice young couple, Brandon and Kerry, just moved in next door, so I walked over to see if they wanted them. Kerry's parents and aunt were visiting and it turns out her parents are huge Sheryl Crow fans. How perfect is that! I can honestly say, my fifteen minutes chatting with them and giving them the tickets was just as happy an experience for me than the concert would ever be. I can see concerts any time. This time, someone else, a true fan, gets to.

As for my breast cancer treatment, I'm waiting to hear when I will begin radiation therapy. I will be nuked five days a week for six weeks (thirty times!) So why the delay? I've been offered an opportunity to participate in a random study that compares photon to proton radiation. Because my cancer was in the left breast, photon radiation treatment may result in the left corner of my heart and lung being radiated, which could potentially cause damage. The simple version is that radiation shrinks and tightens everything it hits, so it could potentially do the same for the portion of the heart and lung in its path (think less pliable artery, tighter lung). With proton therapy, they can control how deep the radiation travels and they can calibrate it to fizzle out before it reaches the heart and lungs (they can't do that with photon). It is a random trial, so I don't know which one I would get, but I don't see the harm in giving it a try and helping out science. Radiation is radiation, in or out of a trial. The best part is, unlike a blind study, once I start treatment, I will know which one I am getting. It's two different machines, so they can't hide who gets proton and who gets photon. As for which form of radiation I end up having, I have no heart or lung problems, so the long-term effects of photon radiation for me would likely be unnoticeable.

One issue with both forms is your basic, or not so basic, sunburn. I liken it to six weeks of abusing one quarter of my body in the sun. Yup, one quarter—sternum to armpit, just below where my breast was to below my chin (half my neck included). In preparation, I am slathering Palmer's Intensive skin care balm on the entire left side of my torso twice a day to super soften and moisturize my skin in the hopes that it will somehow stave off the worst of it. The idea that two weeks in I could start to feel sunburned and have four weeks to go, or worse, the sunburn will get to a point where they decide they can't continue, starts a twist in my knickers if I let myself think about it. Mostly, I don't think about it, but for your reading pleasure, this one time I will.

The only thing worse than cancer treatment is not getting treated. While no one wants to get treatment, once you decide it is in your best interest to have a certain treatment, not getting that treatment feels problematic, like half your troops just left the battlefield for no apparent reason. You can likely replace them, but they wouldn't be your first choice, they would be mercenaries, somehow not quite as trusted and not quite as enthusiastic. It's like calling Wonder Woman and Bat Girl shows up, or ordering a Coke and they only serve Pepsi (or vice versa). Let's face it, no one likes substitutes, and when it comes to my care, I really don't like, or want, a substitute.

But like I said, I mostly don't think about it. I prefer to fan the flames of bliss and bank the embers of worry. Our hammock is still my Zen garden of choice. Something about the way it cradles me, the tinkle of wind chimes in the background, just equals instant relaxation for me. I usually read a book, taking breaks to glance at the sky and watch the clouds gambol by like sheep in a Serta commercial. A giant rubber duck, a man climbing out of a cloud bank, a whale getting ready to slap its tail on the vast, blue ocean of sky, it's all there to enjoy, free of charge.

They serve a purpose, our embers of doubt and worry, loitering in the background, but in the forefront I prefer a roaring blaze of happy thoughts and a menagerie of cloud critters.

Chapter 38 - Stalled in No-Man's Land

Funny place, this no-man's land of waiting. My breast cancer treatment adventure is neither over nor in motion. It has stalled—pick your poison, a bus stop or train station or airport—and I am neither actively in treatment nor free to begin any sort of physical detox or healing process. I'm just waiting.

Okay, somewhat melodramatic, but in many ways true. Chemo is over; surgery is over; radiation is ... looming. I'm waiting, for insurance approval, to find out if I will be accepted into the photon vs. proton radiation study, for this final leg of my treatment adventure to begin so I can immerse myself into it with gusto and zeal and enthusiasm. Once I commit, I commit, and since I have now committed myself to radiation as part of my treatment plan, I'd like to get this show on the road.

Detoxification and healing are tricky processes. They can be hard on the body, just as hard as getting the toxins in was. With radiation around the corner, I don't want to put my body under any unnecessary stress or strain. It's better to wait until all the treatments are done and then move into the healing phase with a clear baseline. I am eating healthy and exercising, a lot, to strengthen my body for the next onslaught, but in terms of cellular detox, that will have to wait.

Patience has never been my strong suit, and breast cancer, well, it will test your patience. Looking back, I do wonder if there were things I could have done differently. Nothing with regard to treatment, mostly with regard to ancillary care. My treatment team covered as many bases as they could, but I am the captain of this vessel, of this body, and there are weak spots that only I know about. So here goes, file this away for future use or pass it on to someone undergoing chemo or surgery, or both. Here is what I would do a little differently, for me:

Dental - Chemo is rough on your mouth. The dry-mouth side effect is bad for your teeth and gums, so if you are cavity prone or have any sort of gum recession, as I do, chemo can do a number on it. The best way to combat it is to meet with your dentist or periodontist before you begin treatment. Go to your appointment armed with what sort of chemo you are getting (the name of the drug will be helpful) and your dentist or periodontist will give you recommendations as to what to do during chemo. If your oral-health doctors don't have any experience with chemo patients, find someone who does. The last thing anyone needs after their cancer treatment is to start incurring large dental bills. Me, I was recommended, and used, an over-the-counter fluoride treatment made by Colgate called Phos-Flur, and had a prescription of Peridex on hand in case of any gum issues. Also, you won't be allowed to get any cleanings during treatment, so be sure to get a dental cleaning in before your chemo starts!

Eyes - Dry eyes is also a side effect of chemo. I used eye drops when my eyes got really dry, but looking back, lubricating my eyes several times a day would have been the better way to go. Get some liquid tears (no Visine!) and use it two to three times a day during chemo. Keeping your eyes lubricated may help slow the progression of cataracts and stave off other eye problems that come with dry eyes and age. It probably wouldn't hurt to make an appointment with your eye doctor prior to chemo and find out what they recommend for you individually as well.

Skin - Your skin is a living, breathing organ (fun fact—the body's largest) that is a crucial player in the body's detoxification process. Post chemo, your skin works hard and takes a beating. The chemo is only actively working during the infusion. As soon as the chemo drugs enter your body, they circulate around, bathing all your cells, and then are expelled through urine, sweat, and feces. You want to make sure this process can happen unimpeded. For the first twenty-four hours, you sweat and pee constantly. It is the body's effort to rid itself of what are obviously harmful toxins. Hydration is key, so your body has the tools it needs to do its job. Dehydration will impede all three detoxification processes. You literally cannot drink enough water. I kept a large glass of water with me all the time during chemo, even a full glass on my nightstand when I went to sleep at night. Not a baby glass, I'm talking like Big Gulp size. Drink, sweat, and pee. Repeat. That is your life for at least the first twenty-four hours after chemo. Embrace it. If you don't like to sweat, get over it, because you are going to. I came to view sweat and pee as a sign that my body was working properly, doing its job. You will feel, well, rank for the first twenty-four hours after chemo, but it will pass. Take a shower the next morning and know that all that rankness is your body doing its job.

On that same front, be nice to your skin. It's working hard. I didn't moisture during chemo (I waited until afterwards; it's a personal choice), but if you are going to moisturize, use healthy products that are toxin and perfume free (Borage is a good one, as are Palmer's products). Choose products that will not clog your pores or sweat glands. A bath can also help pull the toxins out. A holistic practitioner can help you with what to put in the tub to facilitate the process. Always be sure to coordinate whatever you do with your oncologist. The plant world works in mysterious ways.

And so I wait, here on the edge of tomorrow. It's hard not to fall back into old habits of trying to plan my radiation treatments, jigsaw puzzle them into my life, but I won't. This body, this vessel I captain, needs my full attention, and it has it. Once I get the go-ahead, I will be laser-focused on the task at hand, the six weeks and thirty treatments that lie ahead of me. Uncharted water? Yes. Rough seas? Likely. Sea monsters? I can only hope!

Chapter 39 - Where We Find Strength

I wore my wedding ring to bed last night. I haven't been wearing it, not since the weekend I lost it and then miraculously found it when it was turned in to the lost and found at Publix (*Chapter 11 - A Christmas Miracle*). I had planned to start wearing it again after chemo, after my hands stopped being cold and my fingers plumped up a bit in the Florida heat and moisture (sanctioned by my husband), but plans, they just make the universe laugh. Now, with my hands constantly soaked in cocoa butter due to my twice daily scar regimen with Palmer's Intensive, my ring still sits safely in my jewelry box, except for last night. Last night, I had Ken fetch it and put it on my finger. Curled up safe in Ken's arms and with my wedding ring on my finger, the boogeyman seemed just a little farther away.

I've never been good at waiting. When the unfamiliar looms, I prefer to jump in with both feet; to get it done and over with and put the unknown behind me. After my mastectomy surgery, I knew I would have to wait to start radiation treatment, but I had planned on three to four weeks. It was what I was told to expect, it was the standard protocol, and it seemed short at the time. I wondered, worried really, that the scars wouldn't be healed enough, that the radiation would disrupt the healing process and the scars would never heal quite right, wouldn't look quite right, and on and on and on.

My head spins if I let it, powered by a brain that can conjure up scenarios faster than I can stamp them out, if I let it. Sometimes, rarely, I just don't have the strength to stop the crazy (strong word, but it can get, well, crazy). That's when I wear my wedding ring, wrap myself in my husband's arms, and let the tears come. They aren't tears of sadness, they are pressure tears. We've all had them, days when we cry for no particular reason other than the pressure, the strain, has to go somewhere, and so I cry. Sometimes just a tear or two, but I let them fall, without judgement, if they want to, carrying away whatever is eating at me with them.

I could count on one hand the number of times I cried hard during this adventure, and probably still on one hand the times I cried at all. Having never started counting and having never lost count, the more important point is I cry if I need to, I don't if I don't. The tears have no meaning, no definitive game plan or goal, they are just what I do, if I feel like it, when I need to, if I need to, as we all have the freedom to do. Tears, my friends, do not have to signal sadness or that someone or something needs fixing; they are part of the human experience, so enjoy them!

So, eight weeks post mastectomy, I am still waiting to start radiation therapy. Things happen, the drain stayed in an extra week, dragging out the process. I signed on to participate in a study that compares photon vs. proton radiation, which drags out the process. Life, it drags out the process.

The Dummies version of the study I am participating in is that photon radiation waves pass completely through the body and so affect everything that falls in their path. If your breast cancer is on the left side, like mine is, then it may also hit part of the heart and lung. Proton radiation fades as it travels and so can be calibrated to stop (or fade out) when the radiation team needs it to, meaning before it reaches any internal organs, but it will have a greater effect on the skin (also an organ, by the way). The question the study is trying to answer is if there is any meaningful difference in the long-term health and quality of life for breast cancer survivors having had one radiation therapy over the other. Put more succinctly, would not radiating a part of the heart and lung make any meaningful long-term difference.

It sounds like a no-brainer. Who wants their heart and lung radiated? There is still a larger question, though, with an unknown answer. Long term for a breast cancer patient, will it actually matter one way or the other in terms of quality of life or health? That, my friends, is not so much of a no-brainer. While photon therapy may affect the heart and lung, proton therapy is much harder on the skin. Since it has to get to a certain spot under your skin to kill any potential cancer cells, it is more intense on the surface than photon radiation would be, and so potentially more damaging to the skin. In reality, you are swapping the risk, one organ for another. Playing favorites, if you will. Sure, heart and lung vs. skin sounds obvious, but nothing is ever that black and white.

What if I said you could avoid radiating an area that represents one-one hundredth of your heart and lung vs. one-fifth of your skin surface (teeny tiny bit of the heart and lung versus large portion of skin).

Hmmm.

And what if I said, heart and lung problems only occur if you radiate a large portion of your heart or lung.

Hmmm.

And down the rabbit hole we go. You almost need to be a radiation oncologist, cardiologist, and pulmonary specialist rolled into one to make the correct call, and even then there are no absolutes. My golden rule—ask questions, ask more questions, don't ask the Internet.

That's right, don't ask the Internet. It will paralyze you with fear, make you doubt yourself and your team and make you question everything you have done and will do. Trust yourself, trust the amazing team you handpicked, and let them do their jobs. And ask questions, and more questions, and more questions. And let the universe decide. A randomized study can be a gift. After my cosmic roll of the dice, I was randomized into getting photon therapy.

Part of me says enrolling in the study has been for nothing. Wasn't the point to get proton therapy? Uh, not really. The point was to be in a study, to help gather data and improve the way breast cancer is treated. To be part of something bigger, more meaningful, than being just another woman with breast cancer. I'm getting radiation one way or another, why not make it count? Sure, maybe proton therapy would help avoid radiation to my heart and lung, but lengthy conversations with my radiation oncologist confirms that given my physiology (concluded after extensive mapping), my heart and lung will get very low levels of radiation and, all things being equal, one cannot definitively argue one therapy to be better than the other, hence the point of the study.

I could force one or the other, back out of the study and insist on proton therapy, but that would be me pretending I know better, which I don't. Someone on the Internet likely thinks they know better, but they don't know me, haven't talked with me for hours, run tests, analyzed my particular body and breast cancer and life goals and hope and dreams like my team has. No, my money, my life, is with them, and the cosmic roll of the dice. Photon therapy it is. Besides, I still have angels on my side, pulling strings and calling in favors, and they, my friends, know better than all of us.

Chapter 40 - Inhale Deeply and Hold

Inhale deeply. Exhale. Inhale deeply and hold. Breathe.

Again.

Inhale deeply. Exhale. Inhale deeply and hold. Breathe.

Again.

It sounds like a breathing exercise, or a meditation of sorts, but no, it's the mantra of my radiation test run. Splayed like a broken scarecrow, head twisted to the right, I lay there for half an hour, being scanned and x-rayed, over and over. They are quite thorough at Orlando Health, getting the settings for my radiation treatment just right, so that the proper bits get dosed and the sensitive bits get missed, if possible. It seems that if I inhale deeply, into all five lobes of my lungs (thank you, yoga!), my heart will scoot out of the way like a good chap and not be, well, radiated.

I have mixed feelings on all this, the nuking of my person. Ken, my husband, tells me that I was squirrelly before my chemo started too (I asked him), but this feels different, I think. I can't be sure, of course, since my short-term memory moved to a cloud bank during chemo and is still sulking there, but it still *feels* different.

For instance, during my scarecrow imitation, halfway into it to be exact, I had a thanks-we're-done-here moment, an overwhelming urge to just get up and walk away. That's a new one for me. Normally I'm rather stoic, I woman up and muddle through, but not this time. I lay there, eyes closed, pain and discomfort free, nestled into my hard scarecrow mold (although getting a tad chilly), when the thought popped into my head that I should run away. Just get up, walk away, run away, get away. I don't know where it came from, why it came at that precise moment, but there it was, a small voice gurgling up inside me, contradicting my six-week life plan, suggesting I just walk away.

As a rule, I don't ignore inner voices, gut feelings, or nagging sensations of any kind. I didn't run away, but I did have a lengthy chat with my inner voice. (I had nothing else going on at the time, just some breathing to do.) The conversation was inconclusive. Inner me couldn't say why I should run away and I really had no great argument for staying other than "my doctor says I should do this," so we were at a stalemate. I stayed, but that's what I do. I stick it out, hang in there, muddle through.

It's not a great feeling to carry into treatment, this growing tsunami of angst. Radiation concerns me. With chemo, I could see it, feel it, wrap my head around it and work with my body to clean it out. With radiation, I am being dosed with the unknown. With an invisible, tasteless, silent bogeyman, that may not show his handiwork for weeks or months or years to come. I'm doing the best I can to prepare myself, asking lots of questions, asking questions about the answers I don't understand. I understand the process, how it works, how it kills cancer. I understand what I should and shouldn't do during the six weeks to help the radiation do its job and help my body stay healthy. Still, I'm nervous.

Logically, I know why I should do, need to do, radiation therapy. There could still be cancer cells lurking. Minute monsters setting up shop, putting down roots, ruining the neighborhood. Diagnostic technology is good, but it can only see down to a certain level. Beneath that size, radiation does its job, encouraging the small cancer cells left behind to, well, die. It's a precaution, a just in case. I could opt out, but I'm not a gambler. I've come this far, done so much; to stop now would be contradictory. I've done the hard stuff with chemo and the double mastectomy; to pass on the easy phase would be ironic. Still, Monday is day one of this new stop on my adventure, and I'm nervous.

I know I can't, or won't, run away from my diagnosis, or the hospital, or the doctors and nurses and myriad of staff who are there to help me and make sure I'm comfortable and come out of this cancer-free and with every chance of staying that way, but when I'm not at the hospital, I can also honor that part of me that needs to run away. When I'm home, every morning, I ride my spin bike through the roads of Italy, mountains of Costa Rica, beaches of New Zealand, it doesn't matter where (BitGym app). All that matters is that for a short time I get to run away, run away fast. My heart pumping, my lungs bellowing, I feel alive and free and healthy. That's right, I feel healthy, and that, my friends, is the feeling I hold on to for the rest of the day. That feeling is something that neither chemo nor surgery has been able to take away, and I'll be damned if I'm going to let radiation take it away either.

Chapter 41 - Treading Water in a Whirlpool

Lately, I feel like I'm treading water in a whirlpool. You know the feeling, when you try to juggle a short-term overload while insisting on maintaining your personal space, and two days into your six-week temporary situation you know that the whirlpool will win. Not today or tomorrow, but sometime during the six weeks, it will win. So you cry. Not a lot, just an occasional tear here and there. It's not really a cry, it's more of a leak. Yes, that's it, you spring a leak. So now you are treading water in a whirlpool, plugging leaks in your dam with your fingers. All I have is ten fingers; that's all most of us has, so I pull my husband into the mix and let him hold me and listen to me babble on about whirlpools while I leak tears all over his shirt. He and I both know this is temporary, the radiation, the tears, the leaking, but we also know there are still five weeks to go.

I don't want to be treading water in a whirlpool, plugging leaks for five weeks. He doesn't want to watch helplessly while I leak. So, I changed my plan. It was a good plan, to be good to myself during these six weeks, to take my time getting up, do some yoga or ride my spin bike around Maui or New Zealand or Maine, and then go to radiation at 10:20 a.m. Traffic would be easier, I would be relaxed, life would be smoother. HAH! Make a plan, I dare you. I didn't count on the fact that, despite what they told me, radiation takes more than fifteen minutes; it takes closer to forty minutes (and really it should). Between the calibrating and x-rays and adjusting and tweaking (and I'm grateful for all that, really I am! I prefer they take their time, get it right and only nuke what they absolutely have to), it really takes quite a bit of time, and it stresses me out. I lie there, the clock ticking, and I think of my job and all the work I need to do in the short amount of time I'm there each day, and it stresses me out.

It was a good plan, albeit a teeny bit flawed. The fact of the matter is, by late afternoon, I start to slow down; my brain starts to fuzz around the edges. You do sixteen rounds of chemo and a double mastectomy with nary a blip and then jump into radiation and see if eventually your body doesn't say "Uncle" too. Not a full "Uncle" such that would grind you to a halt, just a partial, sort of a polite request for a slight slowdown, a breather so to speak. So I dialed my work hours back to six hours a day and muscled on, thinking a little extra time in the morning would do my body good, would do my soul good, would do me good. So far, I've kept it all going, stayed just ahead of the fray, but now I'm treading water in a whirlpool with my fingers plugging leaks and the fray nipping at my heels. Ah, the best-laid plans ...

I moved my radiation appointments to 7:40 a.m. It's just for a week, then it moves to 8:40 a.m. for four weeks. Then I'm done.

I'm a morning person. Now, as my body recovers, I am even more of a morning person. 10 p.m. to 6 a.m. is my sleep window. Early to bed, early to rise, it's my thing, always has been. I wake up at 6 a.m., no alarm needed. I love the morning, the still quiet, the sound of the birds testing out the new day, calling out to whomever will listen, to whomever will join them in welcoming another glorious moment on this earth. It's peaceful, and anything is possible. I'm not going to say this new time will work, or it won't. I'm not going to make a plan. I'm just going to try, to feel my way through and take one day at a time, to welcome each morning with a song and hopefully not end my nights with a tear. In the end, it will be fine. As my wise mother always told me when life wasn't coming up roses, "This too shall pass." And it will.

Thought for the day - *don't make plans against your grain!*

Chapter 42 - Milestones Help

Monday will be my tenth radiation treatment. I will be one-third of the way through. For some reason, with radiation, with a five-day-a-week schedule for six weeks, milestones help. I have four more weeks, and based on how fast the first two flew by, they will go quickly too.

I haven't really written about what treatment itself is like. It's not like me to skate around the edges. Radiation isn't hard, or painful. As always, the people are nice, in this case radiation technicians. Like always, I've gotten to know them (Abbie is very close with her mom and talks to her every day; Joshua likes to go to the gun range and fish). They answer all my questions and have gotten used to the fact that I want in-depth answers, not just the fluffy surface stuff. There really isn't anything awful about it, so here goes, the real deal on my radiation treatments.

The Thursday before I started, I went in for a "test run" where they set me up as though I would get a treatment and x-rayed me over and over from all the angles they would be radiating me from to see how the beams lined up with my breathing. This took about forty minutes. Breathe in and hold, zap. Breathe in and hold, zap. Breathe in and hold, zap. They adjusted me, adjusted the machine, breathe in and hold, zap. It's oddly lonely, being nudged and zapped. I would make a horrible actress or model from the standpoint that I don't really care for being fussed over by strangers. When all the zapping and nudging is done, they have the settings they will use to line me up each day and I'm free to go. Monday I'll be back for day one.

The first week of radiation was the hardest. In the pre-radiation mapping session, they made a mold of my upper body that I lie in each day. It's not uncomfortable, but it isn't plush, either. I'm not very padded, so that doesn't help. The first day, I took off my gown (it's amazing how immodest you become when you have no breasts), lay back in my mold, they put a breathing monitor on my chest and x-rayed the heck out of me, again. They want to be sure that all their settings and calculations are correct and the x-rays will go where they need to be.

Think back to grade school geometry class. There is the torso and the curve of the ribcage and they want the x-ray to hit everything outside of the rib cage and not inside the rib cage, so with me, they zap me from five different angles to accomplish that. The breathing monitor is to measure how much the rib cage moves when I inflate my lungs with a deep inhale. The deeper the inhale, the farther away the ribs move from my internal organs and the less chance they will get radiated. Once they have determined the settings are good, they do the treatment, which in itself lasts less than ten minutes. Most of that time is the machine moving to different positions (you lie still, the machine moves around you). Before each zap, they ask you to inhale deeply, exhale, inhale deeply and hold. I timed the breath holds. The treatment times seem to vary each day, but the longest hold I had was twenty-four seconds; the shortest was three seconds. They did say it wasn't about the amount each day, it's a cumulative process, so I'm sure they have figured out a protocol as to how much to give and when to provide the beneficial effects of killing any cancer cells while not doing painful damage to healthy tissue.

Day two they x-rayed me again. They check, double-check and triple-check, which is time consuming, but in the end I prefer it. Nobody wins with a rushed radiation treatment. I was there for over half an hour again.

Day three, more x-rays. My radiation oncologist, Dr. Tomas Dvorak, tweaked some settings so they needed to implement the changes and do x-rays. I'm there for over half an hour again.

Day four, x-rays again. The final day, I'm told. From here on out I will be in and out. The x-rays are quick, I'm out in thirty minutes.

Day five, no x-rays! I was in and out in fifteen minutes. It kind of made me wonder what I was fussing about. Same for all of week two, which was actually only four days, because they were closed on Memorial Day. Going forward, I'll get x-ray checks once a week, just to be sure things are still lining up, but it should go quickly.

That's it, boring really. As for treatment itself, the first day I felt like I had spent eight hours in the sun sans the sunburn, and the sun. My mastectomy scar felt like it had shrunk a size, not painful but a general tight feeling. Ken drove me to treatment the first day. I had planned to go to work afterwards, but I was exhausted. Maybe it was the treatment, maybe it was the emotional buildup leading up to that moment, maybe it was any one of a million things, but I honored my body and went home. After that, it was fine. I go to work every day. I'm not really tired, I'm not really not. So far, it's a non-event. Here is what helps make it that way:

Water - Drink copious amounts of water. They say you should drink half your body weight in ounces of water a day. For the first time in my life, I do it. I drink water before I go for treatment and I chug about twenty ounces of water when the treatment is over and keep drinking it all day. It's not hard, I'm really, really thirsty, all the time.

Moisturize - Moisturize copiously with good quality, dye and perfume free moisturizer. I use Palmer's Intensive. I slather it on twice a day. My radiation treatment is in the morning, so I bring a jar with me and slather it on as soon as treatment is over. Don't be stingy, this is skin care for compromised skin. Your skin is being given a mega-dose of the sun's most harmful rays every day for thirty days. Give it lots of TLC. Palmer's can feel like it is greasy, but it's not and it won't stain your clothing. I wear a simple cotton tank top ($8 at Target) under my clothes to provide a comfortable barrier between my clothes and my skin.

Emotions - They tell me that radiation takes an emotional toll on you, more so than chemo or surgery does. They say that the daily treatment is harder than the once-a-week chemo or the one-and-done of surgery. I understand what they are saying, but it doesn't resonate with me. Instead, I prefer to think my body knows. I think the sadness comes from the collateral damage, from the myriad of cells sending messages to my brain to send troops to repair the damage done to the healthy cells as part of the treatment process, and the knowledge that I'm going to drop another bomb on them tomorrow. All I can say is, I'm sorry. I'm sorry it has to be this way. The cancer started it, and I'm going to finish it.

Chapter 43 - Monday Is Hump Day

Monday is hump day. On Monday, I will officially be halfway through with my radiation treatments, which means I am headed into the back stretch. After Monday, I am just ticking days off the calendar, eye on the prize, headed for July 3rd, which is my official last day of radiation, barring some unforeseen cataclysmic event that would cause me to miss a day, in which case July 5th will be my last day, and so on. There is no getting out of radiation treatments, not that I want to. In the end, they are helping me, so trying to weasel out of a day of radiation that is supposed to help me live a longer, healthier, cancer-free life is, well, just plain silly. That said ...

Week three is almost over and it is getting real. At the end of week two I started having some red bumps show up on my chest (or lack thereof), and my radiation oncologist, Dr. Tomas Dvorak, said it is the hair follicles getting irritated. No, I don't have hair on my chest, but there are follicles there nonetheless. Now, at the end of week three, I can definitely see a pink tinge to my skin, and those hair follicles are full-blown pissed off. Friday morning after treatment, I noticed the top layer of skin was peeling a little. Not a sunburn sheets-of-skin peel, just a little flaking. I slathered with Palmer's Intensive, as usual, and voila! Flaking gone. Hopefully the weekend will calm things down a little, because Monday I go back under the beam, and the beam has no mercy.

As you may be able to tell, I am in much better spirits. I found a surefire way out of my funk, or to stop my emotional mudslide— I'm nice to strangers. It's simple, really (and something the world could use more of), I compliment people I don't know. It's a game I call "Here's what I like about you." Everything is more fun when it's a game, right? It works really well in the grocery store or walking down the street where there are lots of people available. Most of the time I don't stop, I tell them what I like about them as I walk by. Sort of a drive-by compliment situation. I do it at that moment when I'm in the sweet spot, when I am on their radar, but not the focus of their attention. Clothes and shoes are easy to compliment, everyone likes their dog noticed, kids I'm careful of since by the nature of the exercise I don't know the mom or the child. When all else fails, a smile and good morning, afternoon, or evening is a winner. The smile is key, for you and for them. I have found that if I compliment someone and don't ask anything of them, such as to stop and engage with me, they are more than happy to accept my kudos with a smile and a thank you and move on a little happier for it, as am I.

So why do people care what a stranger thinks? My theory is twofold. First, what we wear is a reflection of ourselves. Everyone puts some effort into their appearance by virtue of the fact that they went out and purchased the clothes and shoes they are wearing and chose to put them on in that combination that day. I have complimented people for the pithy saying on their T-shirt. It touched me in some way (usually humorous as heck), so I let them know, and the circle closed because I in turn touched them. Second, like it or not, the unsolicited opinion of a random stranger holds weight. If I told someone I didn't like their shirt, they likely wouldn't care, but when I tell them I like it, that I get it, that confirms their own belief and so holds weight.

"What I like about you" gets me out of myself and noticing the world around me again, with feedback. The bonus is if I am actively engaging with the world around me, the world notices and actively engages right back. When we are down, our instinct is to hunker down and keep the world out. I say no, let the world in! Wallowing in my stuff never solved anything, especially when I'm wallowing in a jaded pool of woe or anger or self-pity. Nope, get out of the pool, take a walk among the living and productive, then revisit your stuff later. I am guessing you will have a different take on it. I always do. So yes, Monday is hump day, but it's also another glorious day to be alive.

Chapter 44 - Keys to the Filing Cabinet

The mind is an amazing thing. I liken it to an enormous data center, similar to what you see when a television show gives you a glimpse into the bowels of the national archives. Usually those glimpses involve some controversial box of information being stored on a shelf somewhere in a maze of like boxes with the intention of it never seeing the light of day again. For me, though, those glimpses inspire awe. I'm mesmerized by the sheer vastness of the knowledge stored there. Like the national archives, our minds are a maze of stored information, most of which we never access, never call back to the light of day. Childhood memories, seemingly inane daily events, magazine articles, television shows, news broadcasts, song lyrics, what we had for breakfast, lunch, and dinner yesterday, and the day before, and the day before that, precious moments with our children, precious moments with our parents, fights, laughter, and on and on and on. We file it away under a system that eludes us, but keeps perfect order. The information we rely on is at our fingertips; the memories are just that, precious keepsakes that are buried in the back, until we are randomly presented with the key and they are liberated, like it or not.

It has happened to all of us, a random sight, smell, sound triggers a chain reaction and out pops ancient history. Sometimes we hit the jackpot and these unbidden old memories are good ones. For a moment, as this old movie of sweet remembrance plays unbidden for us, we are whisked away to a long-forgotten moment in time to enjoy them again. Wouldn't it be nice if we had the key to where these old memories are stored, knew the secret password to unlock them at will? To that end, I have found the perfect food that will take you back to your childhood, call forth one of these delectable memories with each savory bite. That food, my friends, is a grape. Not just any grape, a Cotton Candy grape.

I'm going to caveat all this with the confession that I don't actually know what cotton candy tastes like. I know what it smells like, a pink, sticky, sugary cloud, but I have no recollection of the taste. I'm assuming I didn't like it as a child as it was not something I ever asked for when in the usual cotton candy haunts. The smell is unmistakable though, and every circus, carnival, and county fair I went to as a child had the scent of spun sugar hanging in the air. Back in simpler times, before frying food became a sport (fried Twinkies, Oreos and ice cream come to mind). Somehow, the taste doesn't matter, because I know what it smells like. When I was a kid, cotton candy was king, its viscid goodness gilded the faces of children and adults alike. That smell, that sticky, sweet smell of fabricated clouds of pink ... but I digress. This is about a grape.

Organic grapes are hard to find, so imagine my surprise and delight when on my weekly jaunt to Costco I saw a sign for organic Cotton Candy grapes. I don't really pay attention to the names of grapes; I just make sure they are seedless. These grapes are green and seedless, so that works for me. I got them home, washed them off and popped one in my mouth. Grapes are irresistible, freshly washed and glistening, my mouth waters just watching them. They call to me, urging me to eat one, but of course you can't really eat just one, or maybe that's with potato chips. Anyway, imagine my surprise when my mind registered not a grape but, you guessed it, cotton candy! I was instantly a child again at a carnival. Eyes wide at the stilt walkers ambling by, lions and tigers awaiting their turn in the single ring under the dingy big top, their roars competing with carnies hawking their sideshow attractions, and the scent of cotton candy thick in the air. Yes, the sweet scent of cotton candy.

Just to confirm I didn't have my wires crossed, I had my husband, Ken, confirm it. The grapes do indeed taste like cotton candy, not just what I imagine they taste like. It's amazing really, the power of suggestion. Every time I eat one (which will be for some time since I have 3 lbs. courtesy of Costco) I can't help but smile inside. Each time I am transported to a new childhood memory that was perfumed by the scent of cotton candy. Atlantic City, NJ (pre-casinos), the smell of sea air as it washes over the boardwalk. The echo of footsteps on the planks, the call of gulls competing with the saltwater taffy salesman, and cotton candy. The circus, where the smell of animals and peanuts offers steady competition, but can never quite overpower the distinct olfactory calling card that is cotton candy. These memories are powerful, and the odd key to unlocking them is none other than a grape. A Cotton Candy grape.

It does make me wonder, if a grape can unlock distant memories of childhood fun, what other keys are available all around me to unlock other aspects of my past? Chemotherapy unlocked a lot of old memories. Maybe it was a byproduct of my body's efforts to rid itself of the poison coursing through my veins, of the constant flushing of my body with copious amounts of water to get the chemotherapy drugs, Benadryl, and steroids out of my system. Or, maybe these drugs are some form of bizarre pseudo–skeleton key, prankishly trying locks as they go, unleashing memories when the key fit.

Chemo knocked some old memories loose, strange memories that would pop up when I least expected it. Like an old movie that I didn't ask to see, a memory would suddenly start to play in the corner of my mind, running whether I liked it or not. Sometimes it was something that I didn't want to see again, but couldn't tear myself away from. At first I tried to ignore them, but after a while I embraced them, all of them, the good, the bad, and the indifferent. I watched them from the perspective of my older and wiser self, learned something new from them, healed that part of me that had turned my back on them.

One day, this year of chemo and surgery and radiation, of tests and doctors' appointments, fears and hopes and tears and laughter, these memories will lie waiting in a file somewhere in the recesses of my data vault, waiting for a key to set them free. When that happens, I will welcome them as old friends. They are me and I am them. Together we made this moment in time. Together, we are making the future possible.

To find Cotton Candy Grapes - grapery.biz

Chapter 45 - Gooey

Gooey. What a great word. The way it feels inside my mouth, puckering as if to kiss itself and then thinking better of it. Not to mention the images it conjures up. Keebler elves pulling apart fresh-from-the-oven chocolate chip cookies, a cloud of chocolaty steam rising from the molten chips to meet their little noses. Saltwater taffy, the long arms of the taffy machine stretching the long ropes of sugary goodness while the sea air salts them to perfection. Caramel, in any form. Yes, gooey, usually attributed to any number of confectionary delights, just did a nosedive in my world thanks to my radiation treatments. Radiation gooey, friends, is not for the faint of heart.

The Cambridge Dictionary defines gooey as soft and sticky. Pretty straightforward, really, as is the current state of my radiated underarm. Without warning, as is usually the case with these things, my underarm decided enough is enough and began to get gooey. In the instance of my skin, gooey is a strange sensation of moistness, absent of sweat. It is a general, well, gooeyness. It is hard to explain. If you have ever gotten a really, really, really bad sunburn, then you will know what I mean. It starts with a strange tacky feeling, like your skin is moist, but it's not. When you touch it, you stick a little, which you shouldn't. And then it gets sore, irritated really, the whole skin-on-skin thing, and then starts the slow, steady climb to getting worse. Rumor has it that it can fester into an open sore. Personally, I don't want to see where this sore underarm thing can take me. I prefer to nip it in the bud, so to speak. An open sore in my armpit, no thanks. Not on this adventure.

I'm usually pretty gung-ho when it comes to the effects of treatments. They are once-in-a-lifetime experiences, sort of get-it-while-it's-hot one-offs. Currently, not so much. Maybe I'm just ready to get off the treatment train. I have the short hairdo in memory of chemo, I have the scars to commemorate my surgery, and I have a wicked sunburn courtesy of radiation. I think I can forego the raw, open-wound portion of the trip. One less excursion won't make this adventure any less memorable.

Back to my gooey underarm. In my case, it is a skin-on-skin thing. The V union under my armpit has become an unhappy one, deciding to take on an irrefutable sulk that is fast headed towards a tantrum. Currently, my underarm is moist and irritated and pretty much hurts 24/7. I spend a lot of time trying to either not move my arm or hold it away from my body so the skin isn't touching. Hand on hip is a good maneuver for this, but also gives me a stern, sulky look to match my underarm's mood. My radiation oncologist looked at my gooeyness last Wednesday and said I am right on track, that I actually look pretty darn good for having been through nearly five full weeks of radiation. Ironically, that made me feel better; a misguided sense of accomplishment bubbled to the surface. I have spent years trying to temper my competitive nature, but still it appears, usually when I need it least. Still, if cancer treatment were a competitive sport, rest assured, I am nailing it.

Still, I'm gooey, and it scares the heck out of me. So does the blackish-blue hue my skin has taken on, where it's not a bright crimson, that is. The landscape of my upper left quadrant, you ask? The edges of the treatment area have what they call radiation dermatitis, which is a fancy way of saying it's irritated and has the rash-like bumps to prove it. That runs along my sternum and segues into just red, a wonderful, vivid, angry red. When that calms down, usually by the evening of treatment, it relaxes into a bluish-black hue. And then there is the deep, maroon irritation of my underarm. Does it itch? You betcha, but I don't dare touch it. I have this irrational fear that if I rub or scratch too hard, I will start an unstoppable molt and my skin will slough off uncontrollably under my touch.

It's a silly fear, really. There is nothing about my skin that remotely looks or feels like it's coming off, but I'm not taking any chances. When it itches, I slather more Palmer's Intensive on it. When that doesn't work, I soak in the pool (salt pool, not chlorine). The pool takes it all away, the itching, the gooey, the weight of the world. I'd spend all day in it if it weren't for the blasted Florida sun. Being outside is like volunteering to sauté myself. I wait until the sun is going down and the house throws a shadow over one end of the pool, when it is transformed into my own personal grotto of solitude. Their time stops and I am weightless, of mind ... body ... and spirit.

I have one more full radiation treatment (Monday), then five days of what is called a boost, where they radiate just the scar line. All I have to do is get through tomorrow. Hang in there, body, we are almost done ...

Chapter 46 - My Mother's Hands

I have my mother's hands. I usually notice it when I'm brushing my teeth, leaned over the sink, one hand on the counter, the other, well, brushing. When my eyes flicker from the mirror to the drain, then to my hand on the countertop. That's when it hits me, I have my mother's hands. They are graceful, slender-fingered hands, ones that belie their strength to comfort, nurture, love. They are with me always, my mother's hands, steadying me as I make my way through the world, giving me strength as I tackle adventures. Our hands remind me every day that a mother's love is planted deep within you, like a seed, and grows with you throughout your lifetime, that when you leave the nest it is firmly rooted and you are never without it. Yes, my mother's hands, they are quite something.

They also remind me that inside me is the culmination of generations of ancestors from all over the world, who through time and circumstances met, fell in love, married, bore children. And those children did the same, as did their children, and theirs, until today, where here I stand, brushing my teeth, gazing down at hands that resemble my mother's, and no doubt generations of men and women before her. Ours are delicate hands, with fingers meant for a pianoforte and needlework, but strong enough to milk a cow or massage the tiredest of backs (I know, I've done both). Resilient hands that rise to the occasion and meet the grimmest of challenges, yet gentle enough to lull a kitten to sleep. I wonder what my great-great-grandmother's hands were like, or if mine were a gift from my great-great-grandfather?

When my brother and I stand next to my mother, it is easy to see we are all of the same ilk. Alone, we bear no resemblance, but together, we are one, bound together by the genetic glue that is my mother. Psychologically and emotionally though, the three of us could not be more different. We are each a culmination of actions and reactions, life experiences that we passed judgment on and moved forward from accordingly. We have each settled into a philosophy of life that suits us, that adds to the unique melting pot of our family and provides one another with food for thought when faced with the oddity of such a diverse mindset.

If you asked me a year ago if I would ever look to my own family for inspiration on happiness, I would have called you crazy. They are too close, I know them too well. I know what is behind their bright silver dollar facades, in the closets where all their "stuff" is tucked out of sight. With friends and co-workers, we don't get to rummage in their closets. Sure, we may get a peek now and then, but we rarely get a full-on, no-holds-barred opportunity to rifle through their muck. We get to see the tarnish, not the rust. With family, we know it all, and if not all of it, we darn well know enough.

Family is the bastion of unconditional love. They listen, call it like they see it, then work it through. They are the keepers of dirty secrets. So now, a year later, for no discernible reason other than I have my mother's hands, I have started looking more closely at where they find their solace. It also seems that it is not so much for me, but for them, because over this past year I have begun to embrace the true entanglement of family, that their happiness is my happiness, their sorrow is my sorrow. So here I am, quite selfishly, looking at what makes them happy, because if they are happy, I am happy.

My brother, Jonathan, spends a lot of time fishing. Me, I get seasick on a dock. No matter, it makes him happy. I can see it in the goofy grin that adorns the photos of his daily catches. These moments of happiness are my happiness.

My mother, Maria, spends a lot of time with friends or at lectures, doing anything, really, that stimulates her, mind, body, and soul. We talk daily, about this and that, nothing of real importance, just enjoying the soul-soothing sound of one another's voices. And then there is Monty, her paramour. Together they seem to waft through life in a cocoon of bliss. It is hard to tell where one ends and the other begins, they are so in sync, so in love. Their happiness is my happiness.

My husband is a still pool with endless depths to be plumbed. Guitars, books, the stars, they are all mysteries to be unraveled. I have learned that the time he spends noodling on his guitar or staring at the stars, watching science programs or buried in a book, these are his solace. These are what feed his soul. They make him happy, so they make me happy.

Then there is us. We inhabit our own cocoon of bliss. We don't finish each other's sentences; we prefer to hear what the other has to say. With my hand in his, there is nothing I can't do. Wrapped in the safety of his arms each night, the world is right, no matter what goes on outside the circle of his embrace. Back to back, we protect one another from the world; nose to nose, we revel in the wonder of one another. Us makes me happy.

Happiness is found within, and reaches out. When you find it, hold it close, but loose enough to let it fly. Nothing is happy in a prison. When we lose interest in the happiness of others, that is when we lose the ability to be truly happy ourselves. That is when bliss eludes us and the ache begins.

I have my mother's hands. They were there in front of me all along. As was her love, that I have always had and will always carry inside me. I have always had the seeds of true happiness, and I can feel them growing!

Chapter 47 – Deep-Space Me

For the six-week duration of my radiation treatment, I put meditation on a back burner. There was just so much time in the day (classic excuse), and I felt that exercise was more important toward keeping my physical health (and sanity) intact, so I made my spin bike my religion and kept my heart and lungs pliable through regular exercise. I suppose one could argue that riding a bike can be meditative, but since I was doing guided tours and cardio training programs that included ducking branches in the forests of Costa Rica, navigating the beaches of Maui or New Zealand or taking in the sights of the Canadian Rockies, I'm going to say it wasn't. I'm not done with my virtual bike travels, but with daily radiation no longer on the agenda, I am reallocating that time to meditation, or what I fondly like to call "deep-space me."

I will be blunt here, I like what is in my head and I like exploring in there. It is my version of thrill-seeking. I am fifty-five years old, so there are a lot of experiences stored away in my "mind palace" waiting to be rediscovered (yes, I'm a B.C.—Benedict Cumberbatch—*Sherlock* fan). Call me crazy, but I find it fun to revisit old experiences, even ones that didn't go so well the first time, and look at them from an older, wiser perspective.

I did some crazy stuff in my youth, or so I'd like to think, but was it really so crazy after all? Or was it just a somewhat more modern version of what my parents did? Looking back, I was pretty darn milk toast compared to what I hear kids are doing today (wow, did I really just write that!), and in another twenty or thirty years what they are doing will seem mild on look-back as well. The moral of all this? Meditation gives perspective. I have found that if I put my preconceived notions about myself aside and look at my stuff with a dispassionate eye, much of the baggage I have been toting around is just dust. There is no substance to it anymore; the perception I cloak it in keeps it alive. Blow on it and it goes away, dissipates into a distant memory that is more worthy of reminiscence than suitcase space.

I began this Next Generation–like exploration of my inner self after my breast cancer diagnosis. I knew that diet and exercise was not what triggered my cancer, so it had to be in my head. We carry so much stuff around for so long, we lose sight of the fact that just because we are used to the load doesn't mean it is any less damaging. It had to stop, so I was on a mission to rout out my demons and cast them away. Go figure, it ended up being kind of fun. Sure, the beginning was rocky. There is always stuff even I didn't want to revisit, but once I did and worked through it and felt a hundred pounds lighter for it, the positive reinforcement was worth the original discomfort, and I was off and running. Also, there is nothing that says that all this exploration can't include friendly events. I have some really fond memories tucked away that I take for a spin now and again too.

What really fascinates me more than anything else is why I remember certain seemingly insignificant blips in time. These mementos from the past must have some reason to stay afloat, because on the surface they are as inane as glass marbles in a bowl. On closer inspection though, maybe each of these marbles has an inner world to divulge (if you ever saw *Men in Black*, you know where I'm going with this), a hidden galaxy waiting to be discovered.

One past memory that hangs around is the buffalo at Old MacDonald's Farm in Norwalk, Connecticut. He must be long gone by now, since I was maybe five years old at the time. I don't know the life span of a buffalo, but fifty years seems like a lot. He was in a large wooden pen, round as I recall, that was just dirt. Looking back, not great digs for a buffalo, but at five, all I really cared about was that he was on one side of the fence and I was on the other. I remember if you got too close to the fence, he would bang his horns against it where you were. I also remember being terrified of him, thinking he could crush me with those horns. Advanced thinking for a little person, but I was pretty tuned in to danger as a youngster, so those horns were on my radar, as was the sturdiness of the fence.

So, here's a thought, maybe the poor dude was lonely. He was alone in there, no one to herd with (buffalo are herd animals). Maybe all the horn banging was just his way of asking, pleading really, for some attention. All we people did was gawk at him through a sturdy fence. Looking at it that way, I'm not afraid of him anymore, I feel sorry for him.

Old MacDonald's Farm was a really fun place, despite the rightly cranky buffalo. It was in business from 1955 to 1979, so my childhood was its heyday. Simpler times, folks. Much, much simpler times. Plus they had pony rides, and I loved any place that could put me near or on a pony.

Grossinger's. My father is Jewish and he took us there when he was alive. I recall watching a man barrel jumping in an ice-skating show. I remember watching a women's swim race in the indoor swimming pool. Again, this is all under age seven stuff, but why those tidbits? I don't recall anything else there, no details, just that I feel like there is something more to my time at Grossinger's, but I can't quite put my finger on it.

I looked up Grossinger's on the Internet to try and jog more memories, but all I could find was a few personal websites, some old home movies on YouTube, and pictures of the now abandoned, decaying hotel. Seeing a part of my past in ruins, overgrown and rotting, is jarring. Grossinger's was a victim of changing times, which is tragic in itself. Like it or not, we live in a society where we suck the very life and marrow from things in our quest for pleasure then cast them aside, moving on to our next fix. The northeast is dotted with defunct structures, white elephants we call them, that were once the jewels of their time. Now, we can't be bothered. We would rather build new than surround ourselves with the memories of joy and love and laughter that once rang through their halls. I get it, the dollars and sense of it, but that doesn't make it any less painful.

Yup, Grossinger's has loosened up a slew of stuff. I have work to do there; time to put in meditating on those feelings, thoughts, emotions.

Glass marbles, mementos of our past. We keep them in a bowl, pretty baubles with no apparent purpose, but if we look at them, peer steadfastly into their depths, we will find so much more. We keep them around, quaint reminders of past events, but they are there, waiting, whenever we want to look deeper. Whenever we want to address our unfinished business.

Chapter 48 - Sweet Sweat

I love to sweat. I don't know why, but there is something about being drenched in sweat after a good workout that is really satisfying to me. I imagine my body, every gland on full open, flushing out toxins I didn't even know I had. Then, after an appropriate cooldown period, I dunk myself in the pool and let the cool, salty water slowly bring my body temperature back to normal as it soaks out any remnants of lingering toxicity. I do a few lazy laps, breast stroke to relax and stretch my chest muscles, then lounge on the steps in the shallow end and take in the day. The sun slipping in and out of the march of clouds, birds warbling background music punctuated by the staccato of a hawk or two, possibly a rogue breeze rustling the trees, carrying the scent of fresh-mowed grass or flowers. It's there, all around me, just waiting for me to notice. Yes, sweet sweat, it opens up endless possibilities.

It is amazing how fast we forget. It seems like just yesterday that I was charred to a crisp in the aftermath of my radiation treatment, unable to indulge in my pool-time reveries. For the first time in this year-plus adventure, I second-guessed a choice. Four weeks in, I felt radiation was a mistake. I even told my radiation oncologist so. I felt like I was permanently damaged, that along with my skin, my muscles were well-done, cooked as it were, and could not possibly recover. The skin on my underarm was sloughing off faster than it could regenerate and it was red, raw, and painful (second-degree burn in my armpit—ouch!). It also smelled weird, like it was unhealthy and on the verge of something that I called "not good."

At that time I truly believed that, but then again, I was also in the midst of what I now fondly call the Silvadene debacle, so I'm pretty sure all that was the Silvadene talking. All in all, let's just say it gave me pause. Now, coming up on two weeks after my last radiation treatment, it is a faint memory at best. My radiation zone is healed, with only the hint of a tan to remind me that it happened. There are, of course, other mementos that I will likely carry with me for life, so let's give them a spin and see if they make or break the deal. First though, the Silvadene debacle ...

Right after my underarm started getting "gooey," I asked my oncologist for a prescription of Silvadene burn cream. It is for healing bad burns and helps prevent infection. Since the skin was coming off my underarm and the new skin wasn't quite ready yet, and since it had the beginnings of a "not good" smell to it, I was afraid of infection, so I figured better safe than sorry. My gut (intuition, sixth sense, third eye, call it what you will) said to just go with coconut oil and call it a day, but I figured I shouldn't play around with this, so I got the cream my radiation oncologist suggested for just this event.

I put the first coat on (it's a cream, so you apply 1/16th of inch on the area and reapply as necessary) around 11 a.m. on a Saturday morning and within an hour I was dizzy and couldn't make it across the room without stopping to bend over and put my head below my waist. Not putting two and two together, I put the cream on a couple more times until I couldn't make it across the room without sitting on the floor for fear I would pass out and get there in a less graceful (and more painful) manner. By the end of the day I washed it off, and Sunday morning I took myself to the grocery store and bought some organic coconut oil. Truth be told, it was much more soothing, doesn't make you feel like you are going to face plant, and is equally as good as an antimicrobial. Plus, it smells like coconuts, so you smell like a day at the beach. Now, my mementos ...

Sweat - I don't seem to sweat in the radiation zone. Strange, but true. When I read about it, it said that sweat gland function should recover in three to six weeks, or not at all, so I'll keep you posted. For now, it is a strange feeling. I ride my spin bike in the garage. It's probably about eighty-five degrees in there, but it gives me a good sweat. Truth be told, it's cooler than riding a bike on the road in Florida, so don't judge. If it is too hot, I have a fan that blows warm air over me to give the full outdoor Florida effect. When I'm done, I'm dripping, except for the radiation zone. It is akin to the Sahara with only a hint of moisture, probably condensation from the moisture in the air rather than sweat from me. One armpit sweats, the other, nothing. Like I said, we'll see what happens down the road. I'm still healing.

Muscle pliability - I'm back to my uber-limber self. Two weeks after finishing radiation, I can bend and twist and stretch my arms any which way I want and I feel no tightness in my chest. Then again, I am always in motion, so my muscles don't really have a chance to get stiff. Add to that I am still very liberal with the Palmer's Intensive, everything is lubed and warm and ready to go all the time. First thing in the morning, I feel as good as when I go to sleep.

Tan lines - Yes, I have a weird tan line, but I only notice it when I'm fully naked and I can see the whole tilted tawny rectangle. In clothes, it's not noticeable. I wore a strappy sundress yesterday and it looked fine. Then again, I heal fast, and when I tan, I fade fast, so I'm not really surprised.

So, two weeks after my last radiation treatment I am fully peeled and almost back to normal. My energy level is back to full throttle, although my stamina is not fully restored. I fade earlier in the evening, needing closer to eight hours of sleep rather than my usual six or seven. My appetite is moody at best, but I am finding interesting ways to make bland food exciting.

The radiation toasted the mastectomy scar to an indiscernible line on the left side, while the right side is still as it was. It all looks fine to me. They are badges of honor. I earned them. I salute them.

When I look in the mirror, I still see me. Nothing has changed. My husband still looks at me with love and adoration in his eyes. Nothing has changed. The cat still curls up with me at night, purring herself and me contentedly to sleep. Nothing has changed.

I had breast cancer. Nothing, my friends, has changed. I am still me, just better, bolder, brighter ...

POST TREATMENT

Chapter 49 - Then Comes Nothing

A funny thing happens after breast cancer treatment ends. Nothing. That's right, nothing. I have been cut loose, ejected from the womb of treatment care to fend for myself in the reality of rebirth into daily life. No more coddling by nurses schooled in the art of critical emotional care. Now it is just occasional follow-up visits with my oncologist and radiation oncologist and the usual series of questions—are you constipated, do you have diarrhea, are you depressed, are you in pain, have you gained weight, have you lost weight, are you fatigued, and on and on and on. To all of those, no, except fatigue. I like to think of it more like post-treatment letdown. There has been all this hullabaloo for a year, then, nothing. For a full year I have been immersed in full-tilt attention and micro-care of my person, and now, as I mentioned, nothing. In honor of my present state, I will call this chapter, "Then Comes Nothing."

One symptom of this wasteland of nothingness that I now inhabit is that I don't have the stamina for minutia that I used to have. Day-to-day drama seems small, very small. It shrank to its current state of inanity when I was in the throes of my adventure, but now I'm home, so to speak, and back to the usual things that people do when they are not adventuring with a deadly disease. Unfortunately, most of the usual daily stuff I encounter still seems small, at least to me. So I ride my spin bike, purge myself of my doldrums with an endorphin rush, and try and think back to when minutia was the highlight of my life too.

It is no fun when you are left to micromanage your own health. I am not a hypochondriac by any stretch of the imagination, but when you had a potentially deadly disease, dodged a bullet and then are left to float in the gossamer of wait-and-see, you really want to catch it sooner the next time, should there be a next time, so you micromanage. Since I don't have breasts to feel for lumps, I am left to scan every other modicum of my body to see what seems out of whack. So far, I can come up with everything if I let myself, but we all know that's the gossamer talking, so I try and stick to things at least loosely rooted in reality.

Did I mention I'm fatigued? I wasn't "fatigued" during chemo or surgery or radiation. I lagged a bit at the end of chemo and was a little limited in movement at the end of radiation due to my charred state, but I wouldn't say I was fatigued. Now, though, I have definitively checked the "fatigued" box. I used to be able to go all day on six or seven hours of sleep. I popped out of bed at the crack of dawn with no alarm clock, eager to get on with the day. Now, I have no stamina. I'm in bed by 9:30 p.m., mostly because I'll fall asleep anyway, so it might as well be in my bed. It has crossed my mind that this might be a bigger issue. It's been several weeks since radiation ended (tomorrow is three weeks). My burns are gone; only a shadow across my chest that wraps itself around my torso and tucks into my underarm is evidence that the event ever happened. Yet, I'm fatigued. Makes you wonder. Well, actually, more so it makes me wonder.

I'm beginning to think I should have blood work done. It won't tell me a darn thing about cancer, because (supposedly) there is no blood marker to detect breast cancer. All it will do is distract me with something to fix, like I need more calcium, then it is back to scanning myself for seeming irregularities. Lest I sound completely insane, I do draw the line. When my lower back hurt yesterday, the hyper-vigilant neighborhood watch now in residence in my mind raised the idea of a kidney problem, but I nixed it. This process of wait-and-see coupled with catch-me-if-you-can has the potential to cross over into the realm of ridiculous, if I let it.

There is nothing wrong with me. That should be my new mantra, but I doubt I'll adopt it just yet. That would be way too easy, and way too dismissive of what I went through this past year to get to this point. Left to my own devices, eventually the minutia of day-to-day life will swell to its former self-important glory and, refusing to be ignored any longer, reclaim its place of honor at the head of my life. Then again, maybe not. Maybe that's the point behind all this fatigue and angst. My mind-troops are in motion, likely trying their best to keep me from being sucked back into the tar pit of quandaries that had commandeered my life on the first go-round.

This could go either way, so I really should pick a side and make a stand. And so the adventure continues. Silly me, imagining it could ever end ...

Chapter 50 - Soy, the Bane of My Existence

Soy. It has become the bane of my existence. It is everywhere, in everything, with an infiltration level rivaled only by corn. It was bad enough when I watched ingredient labels like a hawk for sport, avoiding additives that weren't healthy to ingest in large quantities (okay, any quantity) on principle, but now the stakes are higher. The ante has been raised, and my obsession with soy has been born. For me, a breast cancer adventurer-turned-survivor, I am trying to do everything I can to stymie the survival of any lurking microscopic cancer cells that may have made it through this past year's Armageddon. To that end, I try to eat healthy, exercise daily with copious sweating to flush out my body, and avoid things that make the first two efforts futile. One must enjoy life, though, and while I love the taste of healthy food, I also like to give my taste buds a vacation on occasion and step across the train tracks to the seedier side of food-land. To that end, soy has become, and likely will remain, an ever-present bane of my existence.

So what is the problem with soy? The basic gist of the potential problem with soy is that it contains isoflavones, which are weak phytoestrogens. The jury is still out as to the effects of soy on breast cancer, specifically hormone-receptor-positive breast cancer, which I have, but more importantly, I am on anti-hormone therapy and there is no assurance that those isoflavones won't affect the anti-hormone pills' ability to do their job. Put plainly, the isoflavones could lessen the effectiveness of the hormone therapy. Ergo, no soy, at least for me.

Full disclosure here—there are lots of articles about soy and breast cancer. They are rife with words like "may" and "not clear" and "if." For healthy individuals, good-quality soy can be a healthy food choice. For individuals with breast cancer, soy may also be a healthy food choice. It really depends on your personal situation and level of obsession. Do your own research, talk to your doctor(s), and make a decision that is right for you.

I seem to be a rare individual in terms of my soy vendetta, or even someone who has heard the "no soy" message. Early on in my treatment, I asked my oncologist, Dr. Regan Rostorfer, what foods an individual with breast cancer should and should not eat. The internet is rife with lists of food recommendations, many of which didn't make sense to me. He said to eat a balanced diet of fresh fruits and vegetables, grains and lean meats (no surprises there), but no soy and no fried food. It seemed like an easy task at the time. I don't eat fried food as a rule and I don't eat soy. No particular reason, just that my tofu phase faded in the 90s and I have never been an edamame or soy nut fan. It seemed so simple, until I started checking labels. Soy oil, soy flour, soy lecithin, the list is endless. Cheap and abundant, at this stage in our food evolution, soy has followed the trail blazed by corn and infiltrated most products in the grocery store.

When I first got the no-soy news, I started checking labels just to confirm the absence of soy in my usual favorite "vacation" foods. It soon turned into a quest to find any products *at all* that did not include some form of soy in the ingredients list. The first mind-numbing revelation was that all chocolate contains soy lecithin. Even most of the so-called healthier dark chocolates do. With chocolate off the list, I then crossed off everything with chocolate in it, so no chocolate chip ice cream, for instance. Since soy lecithin does such a bang-up job of making chocolate creamy and delicious, it is also in all baked goods, like cookies, crackers, and cakes. So, in the blink of an eye, I have crossed off the entire cookie, cracker, chocolate candy and bakery section of the neighborhood grocery store as a vacation destination. My curiosity piqued, I moved to the salad dressing section. All the conventional brands—Wishbone, Kraft, Ken's, even Newman's Own, use soy oil. I have been able to find an occasional organic brand that hasn't switched to soy oil, but you can kiss any fantasy of finding an interesting soy-free salad dressing goodbye. Even fresh meat needs to be checked, as I have found some of it packaged in a solution with soy protein.

The last holdout seemed to be the chip aisle, which until recently seemed pretty soy free. Last week I was heartbroken to find that

Wise potato chips now include soy oil as a possibility. Wise Lightly Salted were the perfect chip, until they crossed over to the soy side of the tracks. Which brings me to my next point, which is the label needs to be checked every time you purchase a product, since the manufacturer may change the ingredients at any time. Finally, there are the sneaky labels that don't list soy products, but follow the ingredient list with a disclaimer that the product may contain soy. It's a minefield out there!

Okay, I sound a bit nuts even to me, so I won't get into the fact that shampoos, conditioners, soaps, detergents, moisturizers, beauty products, and on and on and on, now have soy in them. You can even get soy candles. Soy is not as easy to avoid as I thought, but in hindsight I am probably much the better for it. I fastidiously read labels again, which I had taken to only skimming for a time. I have found alternatives to my former vacation foods that suit me just fine, and in reality, I don't really miss anything that I have opted not to eat. I am still interviewing replacements, which is always half the fun anyway. In the end, the important bit is that I opted to take this path of my own volition. It is my choice and mine alone. I am free to read and interpret the soy literature any which way I want, and Lord knows it is open to interpretation. I could have decided soy is not a problem at all, or that the minuscule amount in the chocolate chips in a scoop of chocolate chip ice cream is inconsequential, but I and I alone chose not to. I chose this soy-free path, because I believe that every little bit helps. If staying cancer-free means that I need to forego the ever-widening world of soy, then so be it.

It doesn't mean, though, that I have to be any less miffed at Wise for wrecking what was a perfect potato chip.

Chapter 51 - Monsters under the Bed

I got stuck. After a few weeks of ever-thickening mud sucking at my boots, I was stuck in it, but good.

I like to think of myself as a trooper, as one who slogs through, no matter what. I'm kind of like the postman in that regard, I do what it takes, no thought of wind or rain or sleet or hail, or me. I just do. That did not make me immune to the mud sucking at my boots, or the monsters looking for a way in. Yes, folks, monsters. They are always looking for a way in, or a way out, as the case may be.

Most people don't think monsters exist, but to me and myriads of others out there, monsters are as real as you and I. No, I don't mean the *Monsters, Inc.* variety. Despite how endearing Scully may have been, I don't foresee him dropping in for midnight tea and screams any time soon. I mean the self-made, home-grown, idle-concern-gone-awry variety. Monsters may be metaphorical, but they are no less exhausting than were they here in the flesh. They wear me out. All that skulking and creeping around the corners of my mind, slipping into the shadows of barely remembered ideas, harrumphing and grumbling in barely audible tones about wisps of things I can't quite discern. There is nothing more exhausting than a deep-seated something that wants to come out, but is being held back by another deep-seated something that wants it kept right where it is. So here I sit, on the sidelines of an invisible line drawn in the mud, waiting for something to make its move, to show its face.

I had a lot more patience during breast cancer treatment. It was easier then, when everything was mapped out for me, when I had a goal in hand. Orlando Health is really, really good at the treatment phase of things, and even at making you feel pampered during what can really never be called a pleasant undertaking. I made the best of it, enjoyed the good bits and endured the not-so-good bits. I laughed a lot, smiled even more. Now, I am left with monsters under the bed, the unspoken fears, the un-cried tears, the unvoiced doubts. I locked them away, down in that place we lock things we hope will never see the light of day again, but there really is no such place. At best, it's a temporary lockdown for thoughts and feelings and emotions that need more time to marinate. Well, time's up. The monsters are banging at the gates and they want to come out.

Funny thing is, like monsters under the bed, when you shine a light on fear, it tends to disappear. It vanishes, like wisps of mist in the morning sun. Just once, wouldn't it be nice to check under the bed and see a real monster skulking there? It doesn't have to be a big monster, or a fancy monster, just a monster. Or even a spider would do. Something to justify the personal torment and effort we undergo to keep the monsters locked away. Something that says it was not all for naught.

Ah, the games we play. Hide-and-seek of the self, stashing bits of feeling here and there, marinating what-ifs into monsters. On some level, maybe I need them, a monster here and there, to keep me on my toes, remind me that it wasn't that easy despite the brave face I wore day in and day out. That despite the smiles and laughter, warm cookies and friendly banter, I was being treated for breast cancer, and breast cancer can kill. That around every turn there really was a monster, that a lot can go wrong (and I thank God, the Archangel Gabriel, and anyone else with a hand in such things that it didn't), and a lot still can.

Today, though, is the day to let it all go again, because today is what I have, right here and right now. My amazing husband, Ken; my spitfire of a mom, Maria; her partner in crime and love, Monty; my brother, Jon (aka Neptune); my brother, Danny, and his wife Josephine; my mother-in-law, Connie, whose love I can feel warming my soul even now; and the scores and scores of people who read this blog and can take comfort that a little light, love, and kindness can make the worst of monsters seem a lot less scary.

Chapter 52 - Yoga, Love at First Movement

Yoga. It was love at first movement when I discovered yoga. I remember sitting on the living room floor with Ken (my husband) and a copy of Rodney Yee's *Yoga: Poetry of the Body* book. We took turns trying to mimic the poses, having no idea what we were doing or what the poses were doing for us. Fast-forward ten years, and I have taken scores of yoga workshops and even became certified as a Power Alignment Yoga teacher in my quest to go ever deeper with my yoga practice. Yet here I am, limping half-heartedly through my personal practice, with no oomph, no interest, no connection to it.

My husband, Ken, tells me to give myself time, to not be so hard on myself, but in my mind I can taste the joy my body feels when it is stretching and moving through a yoga practice. I long for it, my body aches for it, yet it eludes me ...

I can feel the poses, or more likely, remember them, back before breast cancer, before my body was always in a state of healing. First from tests, the pokes and prods of biopsies, then from chemotherapy. I did yoga through most of the five months of chemotherapy treatments, only petering out at the end. Movement gave me solace, the feeling that everything was still all right. The palliative drugs they gave me, whether it was the steroids or the Benadryl, I do not know, seemed to loosen up my body in new ways, giving me access to poses I had been struggling with.

And then it was gone. My energy faded, my practice became shorter; until surgery came and my practice was put on hold. My physical practice became solely a spiritual practice, with meditation as my guiding force. Then, during the six weeks of daily radiation treatments, I relied on my spin bike, hanging on to the notion that cardio workouts would keep my heart and lungs more pliable during the treatments, and thereafter. And now here I am, all that is behind me and yoga is calling me, reminding me it is time to get back on my mat, yet it eludes me ...

One thing I learned early on from yoga is that when I am stuck, I need to mix it up. It works with everything in life. If you are stuck on a problem, tackle it from a different angle. Ask a different question, talk it out with an unlikely ear, and keep an open mind. Sometimes, we can get so set in our ways that we can't hear any other answer than the one that has us firmly mired in our self-made impasse. We see no way out. That's when I mix it up. I meditate on it, sleep on it, push it out of my mind so new thoughts and ideas can have room to move in. With yoga, I let go of the reins. Instead of fixating on the notion that my practice isn't doing it for me, I let someone else do the driving. I go to a yoga studio and let myself just be.

I haven't been in a yoga studio in years. Once I developed a home practice, I found it more rewarding to immerse myself in the spirit of the practice I created. I have also never looked for a yoga studio to practice in, they tend to find me. If you put out what you want in a yoga studio, the right one makes itself known. I want a studio that follows the principles of alignment-based yoga (it has its roots in Iyengar yoga) and has a warm community spirit. To this end, Sweetwater Yoga & Fitness kept coming up, so I decided it was time to give it a go. I dropped in for an all-level, non-heated yoga class.

I'll admit, I was a little nervous about the whole thing. For the past month, my home practice consisted of a few spinal balances, a couple of standing poses and then I'd crap out and move to Shivasana (Corpse Pose, lying flat on my back). Fifteen minutes from start to end, with most of it being Shivasana. Now I was faced with an hour-long class. I told myself I would do the whole class, but I would dial it back. I didn't have to be perfect (I have an issue with perfectionism, I own it); I just had to be. Isn't that all any of us can do, just be? I used to know that, to revel in it, that yoga was not about being perfect, it was about just being, letting yourself embrace and enjoy the moment you are in. It's not really about the pose, the pose is just a vehicle to illuminate the bigger picture, that we are all perfect and we are all flawed, they are one and the same, and neither matters. If we can get that, really get it, then we find peace.

A funny thing happened when I went into Sweetwater Yoga & Fitness and sat on my mat, waiting for the class to begin. All that good jujube, that yoga community peaceful, happy essence that permeates everything, got on me too and it was all all right again. The class was perfect, or maybe it wasn't, but for me, in that moment, everything was as it should be. It was no longer about the class, about whether I could or did do the poses, it was about the fact that I showed up. I showed up for the class and I showed up for me. That's all we can do, each and every day, is show up, try our best, and revel in that moment.

I won't sugarcoat the obvious, I still struggle with where I am physically, but if I look at it from a different angle, I am blessed with this gift that is my body. It bears the scars of wars waged and won, it has braved adventures and embraced the bumps and bruises that come with facing challenges. It has survived, it has thrived, because it is a body forged on a yoga mat, and like a warrior back from battle, it is glad to be home.

Chapter 53 - I Can't Picture Myself Dead

I can't picture myself dead. My mother said that to me the other day. Given that she was eighty-nine years young, I was thrilled to hear it! It got me thinking, though. I can't picture myself dead either, which is a beneficial mindset when emerging from the back end of breast cancer treatment. Normally I'm not a fan of exploring what I'm not, preferring to follow the lead of umpteen gurus, self-help masters, and positive-thinking aficionados in holding positive thoughts near and dear. So what if, just this once, I were to veer from the tried and true path and dabble on the wild side? What if I were to explore what I can't picture ...

Right now, I can't picture myself dead, either. It's a black and white concept, you can or you can't, but in the world of breast cancer, or any cancer treatment, the picture can turn Escher-esque in a heartbeat. It's important to hold on to the picture you want, not let your fears take over and skew your bucolic, agrarian, rolling-fields-of-wheat life into a post-harvest apocalypse. Picture yourself alive. Picture yourself as you want to be. Armed with new life experiences, keep the sun shining on your perfect world, but be thankful for the rainy days. Bucolic settings don't thrive on sun alone. They need a healthy balance of sun and rain to make those perfect rolling hills lushly green.

So now that I'm not dead, and don't picture myself that way, the sky is really the limit. Maybe it's because I went for a physical retooling, opting to go sans breasts rather than try and recreate something that could never be the same again. Maybe it's because I found the prospect of navigating the world physically different quite exciting, and still do. Early on I asked a friend for his opinion as to whether he thought I looked odd or not. Facts are facts, I'm as flat as they come. Think pre-pubescent girl flat, that's me. He said no, didn't even hesitate, and the reason he gave was because I've never gone through life leading with my chest. Wise words. (Thank you, Jeffrey!) I try to lead with my head, but since this blog is brutally honest, I will add that I have always been more invested in my legs than my breasts. Not that I didn't have a perfectly nice pair of breasts, I did. They suited me well. I have long, lean legs, though, so they are the first things that get noticed.

More honesty—as I got older, I spent years wearing pants, because my legs didn't look like they used to. They didn't look twenty. How could they? I was fifty! I eventually got over it and am back in sundresses, but I'd been sans breasts less than two months before I was back in a tank top. That was eye opening for me.

Life is about change. It happens all the time, all around us. The seasons change, the weather changes, our bodies change. I've tried to embrace all aspects of my life, never wanting to be older or younger, just marinating in where I was. Sure, I look forward to things, days, and events other than the one I'm inhabiting, but that doesn't have to detract from my current state. I find that in many ways, looking forward to another point in time can enhance the one you are in. If we have nothing to look forward to, then we have, well, nothing. It can be as simple as looking forward to the rain expected tomorrow that will water your garden, or fall because you like to see the leaves change, or the concert or performance you bought tickets for. Firmly moored in the here and now, I like to look ahead and glance back, to see how far I've come and to jazz myself with what's to come. It got me through chemo and surgery and radiation, being firmly in the moment, embracing everything that I was going through, and knowing that time will pass, it's a given, and eventually this will be behind me too.

One thing I learned early on in life is that there is a huge difference between what I want and what I need. Time and time again, when I thought I wanted something to happen and it didn't, looking back, I always found I was exactly where I needed to be instead. Every job I didn't get cleared the way for a better one; every relationship that didn't work out cleared the way so I could marry the most amazing man in the world (for me). Even having breast cancer has opened me up in ways I never imagined. Day in and day out, I have experiences that give me pause to consider what orchestrations the universe went through for paths to converge, for lives to be touched. That's when I thank my lucky stars I've learned to get out of my own way, to let go of the reins and give life the freedom to run free, run wild.

No, I can't picture myself dead. Who has time for that when there is a great, big, wondrous world to experience, one delicious moment at a time?

Chapter 54 - No Guts, No Glory

The worst thing about breast cancer treatment is the aftermath. I think I'm fine, getting back to some semblance of normalcy, and then suddenly I'm off balance again. At first it's a small bobble, the warning shot over the bow, and then my vessel starts to take on water. No amount of bailing seems to help as some unseen force that seems to know better saps my strength as rapidly as I try to prop myself up. This invisible take-a-break enforcer reminds me, quite forcefully, that I am no longer as durable as I once was. I need breaks, I need rest, I need to forgo some things in lieu of others. I can no longer "do it all." I have to make choices. I like to blissfully pretend that bobbles are no big deal, but even that is nearing the end of its shelf life. I am tired. Tired of being tired. Tired of the aches and pains that come with rebuilding a life that was perfectly fine, but slipped through my fingers.

Quite the sob story, isn't it? It's helpful to cry in your milk now and again. To get it all out, then move on. My dilemma is I like structure and routine, but my new physical self requires flexibility. I took some large strides toward acknowledging some of my limitations over the weekend and I think the latent emotional impact has taken a bit of a toll. You see, I parted with my beloved Mini Cooper convertible over the weekend. It was fabulously fun and giddy-inducing to drive. I loved long trips (and short ones) in that car, just putting the top down and feeling the wind in my hair. I could chart the trip to Palm Beach County, where my mother lives, by the changing scents in the air. The sweet smell of orange groves, the musky aroma of cows and pasture grass ... it was all good, it was all heavenly. And that chapter is now closed. I can no longer be in the sun, so putting the top down is moot. Also, the car was nine years old and I was concerned about getting stuck on the road for any length of time, as I can no longer physically take the blistering Florida heat. I had experienced a few near-miss hiccups as of late, so the prospect of a long trip in the car had me concerned. A found-on-road-dead scenario (the car, not me) would set me back on what is already a wobbly path and, as heartbreaking as it is, I just couldn't take that chance. So, last Friday I bit the bullet and went window shopping for cars.

Who am I kidding, I went car shopping. I almost didn't go, because deep down I knew what going meant, but I forced myself. I did the grown-up thing and took care of myself even though the kid in me was screaming and crying. Sometimes you have to do that, you have to do what is best rather than let your emotions carry the day. In reality, just like me, my beloved old Mini Cooper convertible wasn't what it used to be. It was time.

When you do what's right, the universe throws you a treat. In my case, it came in the form of an island blue Mini Countryman. Some backstory here, I drive a stick shift. It's hard to find those, as most cars on a lot are automatic, so when I narrowed down the model I wanted to a Countryman, I had four stick-shift cars to choose from. One was a 2016 black showroom model customized with a lift kit that would have been perfect for my husband, but wasn't really me. The second was a 2017 red John Cooper Works model, which is akin to an SUV rocket ship. Since I am a bit of a speed demon on the highway as it is, that had disaster written all over it. The final two were 2017 models in green and island blue.

My husband was surprised when I took him to Orlando Mini on Saturday to vet what I had chosen. I was going from a bug-sized sporty car to a four-door car with trunk room. When he saw it, though, he really liked it. The car has that certain something, a personality that calls to me, that says "I get you, let's go have a different kind of fun."

And so a new chapter has begun. I'm not surprised. Last weekend, as I soaked in the pool chatting with Ken, I got the strange sensation that something was watching me. A quick glance at the sky outed the culprits. Dragons. Everywhere! Big ones, small ones, young ones, old ones. One, jaws agape, flashed rows of dagger-sharp teeth; another peered tentatively from behind the safety of his cloud haven, wisps of pipe-like smoke teasing from his nostrils. One stood boldly, full body in view, peering down at a small dog yapping up at him. It reminded me of a Sandra Boynton pillowcase I have with a picture of a tiny knight wielding a tiny sword on it. He is staring up at a friendly green dragon who, neck arched, peers down at him. The slogan is, "No guts, no glory." That about says it all.

Chapter 55 - Muscle on My Side

Is it odd that I view the sky as my own personal divination tool? All I have to do is glance skyward to see the echoes of my path unfold. Yesterday, lounging on the steps of the pool, I watched as giant, billowy superheroes scaled banks of clouds, on the ready for what may come. Their determined gazes shone through slits in their helmets, their muscular forms were poised and ready, awaiting a command, from me maybe? They were comforting, in an odd way. I have muscle on my side, even if it is only a reminder that the muscle on my side is me.

Too often we forget how capable we are. After one year of leaning on my husband, of letting his strength support me in ways I never even knew were possible, or that I ever imagined I could ever need, the time has come to take off the floaties and swim on my own again. These tentative first strokes are hard. I have to keep reminding myself that no one is abandoning me, that I am perfectly capable, but it is still hard.

Truth be told, all that attention was kind of nice. Oh, who am I kidding ... it was great! As a strong, confident woman, I have spent my life being leaned on, helping friends and family navigate the hiccups in their lives. This was a new experience for me, being the leaner, and it did not come easy. It was hard to let go, to turn over my emotional and physical well-being to the care of someone else, but I do have an awesome husband (Ken), and he made it easy. He stepped in with seamless ease, slowly easing the burden without my even realizing he was doing it. Before I knew it, he was my life coach through all this, my strength, my rock, and I never saw it coming. I also never saw it coming that bouncing back from treatment, both physically and emotionally, would be more like riding a Pogo stick than a gradual ascent. Ken is still there, though, dusting me off when I stumble and encouraging me when I balk.

Balking is easy. There are a million reasons not to follow through with my new regimen, which are all new and different reasons than if I were not recovering from breast cancer treatment. For instance, as much as I love yoga, I get tired. Not just tired, but out-of-gas tired. I don't know if you know the feeling, but it's like you are literally out of energy and your body is in safe mode and all you can do are the basics, like walking and talking, because there is nothing left for more than that. It's not a question of actual fuel, like food, there just seems to be a limited amount of energy I am allotted for fun stuff, like movement, and the rest, I hope, is going toward rebuilding my body. True, I would squander all that energy, given the chance, on never-ending yoga practices, letting soft, acoustic indie music guide my movements, and so I am not allowed. Thirty to forty minutes of gentle practice is all I'm good for. When my energy is out, I putter to a halt and no amount of desire can get me moving again.

I still have trouble getting through a full forty-hour work week. I go to work every day, but it is healthier for me if I work six to seven hours per day, rather than eight hours. I don't know why, it's just one or two more hours per day, but it seems to make a huge difference. If I work a full forty-hour week, then I'm worn out by Friday and not even the weekend can make it right. I enjoy my job, so the short hours aren't doing me any favors on that front. I work for a nonprofit and we do interesting, meaningful work. My body doesn't care. When it is out of energy, it's out of energy.

Don't get me started on soy. The problem with any strict dietary measure isn't now, it's later, when you feel better, or fine. That's when you are tempted to cheat. At this point, I'm so irritated by the proliferation of soy in our food supply that I won't eat it on principle alone. Hopefully that feeling will last and carry me through any weak moments that may arise.

One of the amazing things about yoga is that it not only adapts to every person, it adapts to every time in your life. For now, I am keeping my yoga practice to about forty minutes of what I like to call "joyful flow." I am not focused on getting stronger or better, I don't worry about trying new or harder poses, I just move.

I like to practice yoga first thing in the morning, before the world wakes up. I like the silence. Not just the physical silence, but the emotional silence. We all exude energy. We think that the frown on our face is the extent of it, that the worry that creases our face is ours alone, but not so. The anger or frustration or worry we hold inside, we send it out there; it is our energetic signature. First thing in the morning, all that energy is asleep. All I feel is the balanced energy of nature, of the plants and animals. Leaves rustling in the breeze; songbirds greeting the day; maybe a hawk waiting for its next meal. There is no anger or frustration, just the wheels of life turning. And so I join them, slowly waking up my body, reveling in the wonder of movement, in the joy that is the physical body that I am blessed with. And I am reminded, inside me is a superhero.

Chapter 56 - Thank Your Guardian Angels

Fear is a funny thing. Sitting smack-dab in the center of Florida, I have obsessed over Hurricane Irma's drunken-sailor progress this past week; first her westward trek across the Atlantic, then her indecision as to when to turn and where in Florida to make land. She is as indecisive as to her landing point as I am with the TV remote. Hundreds of channels and not a thing to watch. I get it, her wishy-washy swish across the Atlantic, but indecision makes me nervous. I like certainty, outcomes I can wrap my head around. Since predictability is never an option with a hurricane, or any natural disaster for that matter, when trouble looms, I send out a bat signal to my guardian angels and thank them in advance for getting me through this, too. I say "too" because they were all there at the forefront for my year of breast cancer diagnosis and treatment, and they will see me through this as well.

I am always amazed at the guidance I receive from my guardian angels. It is subtle, but if I pay attention, they come in loud and clear (their voices can often be mistaken for thoughts). For instance, as of Friday (yesterday) morning, we had no plywood to board up our house and no prospects of getting any. After wallowing in despondency for an appropriate amount of time, I took a deep breath and asked for help. "Where can I find plywood?" I asked whoever might be listening. Lowes and/or Home Depot were obviously not the answer. Clear and concise it came to me (angels don't mumble)—a lumber yard. I did a quick Internet search for lumber yards in Apopka and the first one that came up was Hood Distribution in Lockhart, Florida. I called them and, despite being a wholesaler, they had opened their doors to the general public that day and were selling plywood to homeowners who needed to board up their houses. I bought fifteen sheets and, while I waited for Ken (my husband) to show up with his pickup truck, struck up a conversation with the branch manager. He shared with me that they were making plywood available to the general public because it was "the right thing to do." The price was the same had I gone to Lowes or Home Depot. Bottom line—he had wood; people needed wood. It was as simple as that. It was the right thing to do, and he did it. And my guardian angels connected me with him. After Ken got there and loaded the wood, I went over to the branch manager to say goodbye. We hugged, told each other to stay safe, and I kissed his cheek. It was the right thing to do.

I try not to read the Hurricane Irma news, the predictions and discussions and commentaries. Some days I am more successful at it than others. Irma is fast reaching celebrity status, reaching for records set by Hurricane Andrew and others before her, and everyone is talking about it. How could she know Tampa hasn't had a major hurricane since 1921? Yet now she is headed that way, her wobbly plod becoming more sure, more exact.

It is times like this that my practical side takes over. Irma is a storm, a product of nature. It is the birth child of warm water, wind, and delightful weather twelve months a year (grossly over-simplified, but if you want the whole conception story, go to https://scijinks.gov/hurricane/). The joy of wearing shorts year-round comes at a price, and the price for a Floridian is the possibility of a hurricane. The spit of land our homes inhabit hangs out into the Atlantic like a pinball machine flipper, a perfect hook to catch every storm the Atlantic births and sends careening in our direction. In these instances, we have no choice but to tap our guardian angels on the shoulder and ask them for help.

While I don't believe even a guardian angel can change the path of a hurricane (it would be hugely unfair to those residing wherever it ended up making landfall, not to mention a gross violation of some sort of guardian angel code of ethics), they can help you weather the storm. So here is a great big thank you to all the guardian angels out there, watching over their charges in Florida, the United States, and the world. Whether wind, rain, fire, or snow, mudslide, tsunami, or earthquake, there is someone there looking over our shoulder, tipping the scale a smidgen this way or that. It may not seem like help at the time, but the alternative could be a whole lot worse. Sitting here in my boarded-up house, I know in twenty-four hours the wind will be howling. I'm grateful for these serendipitous boards of wood between me and whatever the wind may decide to play catch with. I'm grateful for my guardian angels and the little things they orchestrate that end up making a huge difference.

Chapter 57 - Stress ... Free

Hurricane Irma has come and gone, but the stress lingers on. A quick look at the National Hurricane Center website shows José, Lee and Maria making their way across the Atlantic, reminding us that hurricane season isn't over quite yet. We must sit tight, wait and watch, while these children of the Atlantic cavort about and decide what path to skip down next. Like bullies in a playground, they taunt and tease; they harass us with the threat of wind and rain, rip tides and storm surges, and all we can do is hope they opt to play elsewhere.

And that is one of the myriad of reasons I do yoga and meditate. I find the threat of home-destroying winds followed by the possibility of weeks with no power (aka no air conditioning) in the height of summer (imagine your house has become a sauna) to be, well, stressful. Having dodged a bullet with Irma (thank you, thank you, thank you, oh guardian angels, angels of all kinds and the forces that be in the universe, for letting us keep our power!), I am now focused on the reloaded gun pointing my way. I find it, well, stressful, that three hurricanes are meandering around out there, and hurricane season doesn't end until November 30. Yup, I find that really, really stressful.

To combat the stress, I went to gentle yoga this morning. The magic of yoga is that the poses are designed to calm and balance your nervous system. I don't have to do an extreme practice, to come away wrung out and ready to drop, to feel calmer. All I have to do is go through the poses, let them work their magic, and breathe.

I know what you are thinking, you feel better when you do an intense workout. Muscles burning, sweat pouring down, not an inch of dry when you finally cry "uncle" and head for the shower. I get it, I was there, and if I still physically could, I might be right there with you (it's a longer-term plan), but yoga is more forgiving.

It works with your body, whatever your level or physical ability, and encourages you to be more, while still letting you know you are completely fabulous right where you are. It works on your stress, just differently. When you do an insane workout, you feel better because you are burning off the adrenaline, letting the steam out of the pot, as it were. Think of a pot of boiling water. Take the lid off and the pot calms down, but the source of the heat is still there, and before long the pot starts to boil again. That's why it takes longer and more intense workouts to get the same effect. Not so with yoga, the poses are the poses are the poses. You can get better at them, get stronger in your execution of them, advance and try more difficult ones, but they still work regardless of your level. They work because of the breath.

With yoga, each movement is married to an inhale or an exhale. Imagine if you synchronized your life to your breath. Inhale, you open the refrigerator. Exhale, you contemplate your options. Inhale, you reach for the orange juice. Exhale, you pour yourself a glass. And on and on and on. Life would be more mindful, more thoughtful. Your actions would be contemplated and sure, rather than a haphazard array of movements, half of them executed on autopilot while your mind whirls about something else. Breathing, we do it every day, over and over, yet we never really pay it any mind. But what if we did?

What if we took a breath before we spoke, took a breath before we made a decision, took a breath before everything? Yes, we would slow down our day, but isn't it the frenetic pace of our day, our week, our lives, that is compounding our stress levels anyway? I think a little mindful breathing would do wonders for the world. Give it a try, maybe in the shower? Or after you get into bed? Or before you get out of bed?

Close your eyes and breathe in through your nose to the count of 3 or 4, or 5, whatever is comfortable for you, then pause, and breathe out to the same count. Repeat this, maybe start with 5 times, or 7 times, or 10 times. Again, what you are comfortable with. Don't think about anything, just breathing. Remember, through your nose. It makes the breath slower. Seriously, how fast can you really breathe through your nose? Think about the air flowing through your nostrils and down into your lungs, then back out again. Over and over, carrying away with it tension, stress, anxiety. If it helps, you can, in your mind, inhale and hold in your mind that you are inhaling calm, then exhale and hold in your mind that you are exhaling stress. Use whatever words work for you:

Inhale ... calm, peace, love, hope

Exhale ... stress, anxiety, sadness

The right words will come to you.

Start and end your day this way and you will feel calmer, more grounded in yourself and more connected to your actions. Whenever you feel stress creeping in, take a breather, literally. A couple of deep inhales and exhales and you will feel the earth coming back under your feet, solid and sure.

That's all it takes, a couple of slow, deep breaths ...

Chapter 58 - Remembering How to Play

When I visit my mother, I do yoga outside on the deck beside the pool. There, the scent of salt spray lingers on the breeze as it moves clean air off the ocean and over the berm of grape leaves, the methodical sound of waves pushing and pulling on the shore keeps tempo with my breath, and my yoga practice goes through a reset. Outside, where there is no mirror to check my form, my practice is more organic, more intuitive. My body remembers how to move without criticism; it remembers how to play.

I have select memories of playing as a child. I remember making mud pies with my childhood friend, Leslie, giving no thought about the effect on my clothes. Today, I can't even cook a meal without fretting about spills and dirty pans, often wiping counters and washing soiled utensils and pots while I'm dirtying new ones in an effort to get dinner ready with as little aftermath as possible. Just once, I should let these mealtime casualties pile up and enjoy the process of cooking, but alas, I am not very adventurous when I cook, preferring tried and true spices to venturing into uncharted culinary territory, so it is easier to scurry about doing mundane tasks to distract myself from my shortcomings. I never had this problem with mud pies. They held my attention fully as I mixed random items I had collected from the kitchen together, willy-nilly, with no investment in the outcome, just in the joy of friendship and play.

I also remember that, as a child, my imagination ran wild, conjuring up make-believe characters that beckoned me to imaginary places for exciting adventures. Who knows how or why this superpower fades, this ability to transport oneself through space and time into the situation of our choosing. I also don't know why, all of a sudden, one day I realized I missed it, the ability to leave reality behind and vacation in another realm, and I wanted it back.

It took work, re-initiating my mind into the world of play. It was so stuffed with the serious business of adulthood and work that the ability to imagine beyond the nose on my face had faded away. It saddened me that the rich playground of my mind had been re-purposed as a repository for the doldrums of day-to-day life. It took a deliberate effort to recapture this childhood ability, and it has paid off. I get enormous enjoyment out of immersing myself into imaginary worlds of my own creation, where the characters are my avatars and their stories are my quests (no, I've never played *Dungeons and Dragons*). Together, my mind and I have amazing adventures; together, we play.

Play is an important part of my mental and emotional well-being. It is an important component of what makes us all human, the desire, and need, to be entertained, to play. Without it, we fade. We become that stodgy person who goes through the motions of life. Ebenezer Scrooge is a classic example of what happens when we let life take over and we make play irrelevant. We are reminded of it each year when *A Christmas Carol* is trotted out and shown in a myriad of versions so it will appeal to everyone (my current favorite is the animated Jim Carrey version). When we play, we infuse color into our lives, adding a vibrancy that rubs off on even the mundane bits.

So, having mastered play in my mind, it never occurred to me that there was more, or that I might need more. Then I met Jennifer Schelter. I got to know Jennifer when my husband, Ken, and I, attended her Radiant Retreat yoga retreat she holds each March at Maya Tulum in Tulum, Mexico. Jennifer is an artist, writer, life coach, and yoga teacher. She pours her enthusiasm and zest for life and all its wonders into everything she does and she is adept at melting the shell of adulthood that hardens us into our stodgy ways. Jennifer introduced me to the concept of play in yoga.

So, what is play in yoga? For me, it means smudging the edges, coloring outside the lines, messing around. Play gives me permission to put my own spin on things, to get creative and turn my practice into a reflection of my spirit. My yoga practice is always freestyle, choreographed as I go to express what I feel and need at that moment. For instance, this past weekend, the warm sea breeze nudging me along, rather than focusing on the poses, I shifted my focus to my body and imagined my body parts as members of a team. With childlike wonder I was riveted to the placement of my hand, the spread of my fingers, the hug of my palm against the earth; then my foot, the feel of my toes stretching out along the ground, the solidness of my heel on the earth; the subtle muscular adjustments in my foot and ankle in tree pose that allow me to balance seemingly effortlessly; the release in my waist that allows my torso to rotate just a little farther in revolved triangle; the lift in my core that keeps me buoyant in crow pose. Every movement was more giddy-inducing than the last! When I think of the thousands, if not millions, of minuscule course corrections by muscles and sinews working in concert that keep me upright, never mind twisted into a yoga pose, I am in awe. I also can't help but want to take this fantastical body I get to inhabit for a real test drive. Like a teenager given a chance to sit behind the wheel of a Ferrari, I am eager to see what else it can do, and so the play really begins.

Play comes in many forms. For me, it is through writing and yoga, for another it may be something else. Sometimes it is as simple as doing a common activity differently, or looking at something in a different, more childlike way. Forget what you already know, that you have done something hundreds of times. Look at it, experience it, as if this is your first time. If you love to run, get off the road and run through a nature trail. Visit a zoo and feed the giraffes. Go to a science center and play in the hands-on room. Drink hot chocolate in bed, or stomp in a puddle. There is no right or wrong. It's play! Anything that gets you out of your well-worn rut will do. It is never too late to reconnect with that place in you that knows how to play, that place that knows no bounds and isn't wrapped up in the trappings of life.

And no, it is not immature. It is play. Give it a try!

Chapter 59 - It's Technically Not a Spa

Wednesday, I am going in for some touch-up surgery. They call it
a scar revision, I call it the removal of my man boob. Okay, not
politically correct, but that's what it is, a small amount of fatty
tissue that was left behind and has taken up residence as a small,
slouchy, pseudo-breast. Not a woman's breast, not the sleek twin to
its chest-mate that it is supposed to be, but a man boob. There are
several emotions that have come up and been mollified with logic
over the fact that I am going back in for surgery, so hopefully you
will find them as amusing as I have, and possibly useful -

Never say never. I always told myself I would never get any sort
of cosmetic surgery. I'm not vain, so my philosophy has always
been that aging is a part of life; embrace it, accept it, enjoy it. That
was before having breast cancer. The decision to not have
reconstructive surgery was an easy one for me. I prefer physical
ability to attempting to retain a form that won't exist anymore. That
was my take and my choice. Everyone is different and every
decision has to fit the person. That's why they offer options
(although going flat is an option you have to research and come up
with on your own). That said, here I am, looking down the barrel at
elective cosmetic surgery. Like it or not, I can exist with my man
boob. I am having cosmetic surgery. Maybe not the most
conventional of cosmetic surgeries, but it is cosmetic nonetheless.
Touché. Never say never.

How could the doctor have missed that. That was a tough one to
wrap my head around, sort of. I am eternally grateful to Doctor
Jeffrey Smith for all he did for me during my double mastectomy
surgery. Going into surgery, we both knew my priorities. Breasts—
lop them off; lymph nodes—move heaven and earth to keep as
many as you can. He saved my lymph nodes, which is what I
asked him to do. He knew how important it was to me for there to
be as little damage as possible to the delicate lymphatic
infrastructure of my body, and he did all he could to accomplish

that. (He ended up only taking three lymph nodes.) I know that wasn't easy. (Did I mention I was eternally grateful?) Yet, here I sit, daring to entertain the slightest smidgen of disgruntlement. Deep down, I know he was kind of busy doing all he could to accomplish what mattered to me. My dear friend, Sammy, brought it on home, though, when she said, "He was too busy cutting the frigging cancer out of your body." (She used a stronger word.) The moral here—stick to your priorities and don't sweat the rest.

Crap, there will be needles. I went to my pre-op appointment this week and they took blood, and I was instantly reminded that I don't like needles. I don't like blood being taken out of my veins and I don't like things flowing into my veins (oddly, not the same reaction with a port). I've always been that way. I know they don't take a lot of blood (they took two vials), but to me it feels like my life force is being drained away. I can't watch, or I'll faint. Hell, I can't think about it or I'll faint. And it's not just a small prick, I can feel the needle rattling around in my vein when they change vials. I don't say anything, I prefer to just let them get it over with. Yet here I am, several days out from having a large needle take up residence in my forearm for several hours. There is no getting around this, there will be needles. Crap.

It's technically not a spa. I love Orlando Health. When I think of surgery (I had two—one to put in my port and one for the double mastectomy), I think of warm blankets and leg massages and smiling faces. It's like a spa day, but it's not. It's waiting around for your surgery. Since I don't go to spas, though, this is as close to a spa day that I've ever had, so it's a spa day (but really, it's not). Hmmm (light bulb)... maybe I should go to a real spa and have a real spa day.

So here I go, to the spa that is not a spa, for cosmetic surgery that I said I would never have. It doesn't bother me. Long ago I realized that to really live life, I have to embrace what is going on right now. For me, plans are a loose approximation of where I might like to find myself in the future. Next week, I will find myself among old friends and a group of people that care deeply for my comfort and well-being. The path is laid, the destination is clear. Onward Ho!

Chapter 60 - Man-Boob Removal Day

It is done. My man boob is no more. In its place is a line of steri-strips and thin plastic tubing draining off any excess fluid that could build up and hamper the healing process. I am an old hat at this, emptying the bulb twice a day, recording the fluid levels. Like the first go round, the right side doesn't drain much and has already trickled to almost nothing. That means on Thursday, the drain will come out and the steri-strips will be removed to reveal a pink line of healing flesh. But I'm getting ahead of myself. Here it is, a blow-by-blow of man-boob removal day:

Ken, my husband, got me to the hospital at the respectable time of 9 a.m. in preparation for my 11 a.m. surgery. It sounds like a long lead time, but it flies by. Any wrinkle in the fabric, any ripple in the flow of events and BAM! I'm off schedule. When that happens, it reminds me of a barnyard, where everything is calm and idyllic until suddenly it's not and the chickens start to scurry around, clucking in indignation. Nurses don't really cluck in indignation, but they do begin to eavesdrop on one another, ready to swoop in at a moment's notice and help any process that is drifting sideways get back on track. For now, though, I'm still in the waiting room, holding Ken's hand and wondering if I have time to go to the bathroom one last time.

It works every time. Whenever I'm waiting for something to happen, or in this case, for a nurse to come get me and bring me into pre-op, if I go to the bathroom they will immediately appear and call my name. No sooner did I get into the bathroom when I heard my name called. It does beg the question, why would I want to hurry things along? In my mind, I'm playing beat the clock. The vein debacle of March 20, is still fresh in my mind (*Chapter 31 - The Art of a Happy Surgery*) and I don't want a repeat, so I figure the less time my veins have to dehydrate and become problematic, the better.

Leaving your husband in the waiting room is the worst. I want him to come with me, to be the calming force that is smiling beatifically by my side while I prep for the slice and dice, but that's not how it works. I have to do this march alone. Only when I'm scrubbed and primped and pricked does he get to come in, get to be the after-the-fact bastion of comfort that calms me when I'm likely already uncorked.

A quick rundown on the prep march-

First stop, they take me to the bathroom (ironic, right!) There, I swab the edges of my nostrils with iodine solution, twice each nostril, brush my teeth, and swab the inside of my mouth with disinfecting mouth rinse, then finish it all off by rinsing my mouth with the leftover mouth rinse for thirty seconds.

Next stop, they take me to my bed. It's a cubicle curtained off from the others for privacy, of sorts. They rifle through some release forms, have me sign my fate away to surgeons and anesthesiologists, review my allergies with me again, then curtain me off to strip and wash.

Orlando Health takes their cleanliness very, very seriously. I've already washed twice with disinfectant wash at home—once the night before and once the morning of surgery. This is the final scrub down, for good measure. In case you are wondering, yes, all that antiseptic wash does make you itch, but that's the least of my worries. I'm still thinking about my veins, so I strip down to my underwear, pack my clothes and shoes away in the plastic bags they provide and scrub myself down with the thick, warm antiseptic wipes, one for each arm, each leg, my front and my back (think the size and consistency of Swiffer Sweeper Wet, and yes, they warm them up for you). Then I slip into a gown and prostrate myself on the bed (think Victorian bride on her wedding night).

Next comes the blood pressure cuff, the oxygen monitor on my finger, the leg massagers to help with circulation and a slew of arm bands to identify the critical tidbits of my medical persona should someone need to know them stat. A nice, warm blanket tops off the package. I do find watching the monitors entertaining. Slow, deep breaths and my blood pressure drops; my nurse shows up to put the IV in, my blood pressure does an about face and heads for the top of Mt. Everest.

I'm not a fan of needles, or IVs, or anything that punctures my veins. I don't like the feeling of blood coming out, unknown liquids going in, or in general thinking about the fact that there is a sharp metal object lodged in my arm. Be that as it may, I signed up for this trip, and to get where I need to go, an IV is a necessity. Still, me being me, and me having been there when the IV debacle went down at my mastectomy surgery, I thought some helpful pointers would be, well, helpful, so as not to have a repeat of what I would prefer to be a once-in-a-lifetime experience.

Nurses don't like pointers. I get it, who wants a patient telling them where to put in an IV. In my defense, I explained the why and wherefore of it all to her, although I didn't go into the fact that I have a habit of being right. I also didn't say "I told you so" when I was right. I simply told her what happened the last time I had surgery, offered that the higher up on my arm the better in terms of success, and she just smiled and said my veins look good, she doesn't feel a valve that could interfere with the IV, and off she went. The IV went in "beautifully" (her words), and then sprung a leak equally as beautifully. She took the IV out, put a pressure bandage on the hole so the blood wouldn't pool into a bruise, and began to feel around on my hand, at which point I quite sternly said "get my husband." I must look scary when I'm stern, because the nurse in the next cubicle scurried off to get Ken. He arrived, smiling and cheerful, and to his credit, his smile never wavered, even though I'm sure inside he was having an oh crap déjà vu flashback similar to mine.

Maybe the presence of my handsome, strapping husband swayed her, or maybe she just figured that maybe I really was right, as the nurse opted to go higher up on my arm and, thankfully, the IV went in and stayed in. Still, it does make me wonder. I've never had a problem with the quality of my veins before, maybe the chemo did something that has not righted itself yet. Another rabbit hole to lose myself in, but that's for another day.

There is something anticlimactic about this surgery. It is not lifesaving, it is merely making my already flat chest even flatter. In my head, I understand why I am doing this. My husband is afraid cancer could grow there; I doubt it, as it is not breast tissue, it is fatty tissue. For me, the minuscule shred of vanity that runs through my DNA would prefer symmetry to lumpy. I didn't want to spend the rest of my life dressing in dark colors or patterns that steer the eye away from my lumpiness, when I could easily fix it and create a smooth, flat canvas from which to paint masterpieces. I wrestle with the idea that this was silly to do, but I am also glad it's done. A month from now, it will be ancient history. A month from now, I'll be wearing pastel.

Chapter 61 - Happy Anniversary to Me

Happy Anniversary to me! One year ago, I posted my first blog post, "I'm Happy, Really, Really Happy. And Oh, I Have Breast Cancer." What started out as a way to communicate with family and friends about my "adventure" with breast cancer became much, much more than that, and I thank everyone out there around the world who is reading and sharing my thoughts and ideas on how to navigate life when you are handed a bucket of lemons. Now, one year into this adventure and closing in on looking at it from a rearview mirror perspective, I feel like I've left the oasis of treatment and am faced with an endless sea of sand in every direction. I know that somewhere out there is the other side, that if enough time passes, chances are I'm in the clear, but I also know that the next few years will be fraught with conflicting information, missed opportunities, wrong turns, and backtracking. I also know that I'm not alone, that anyone who has had a serious illness or medical condition has likely walked a similar path and stumbled up against the same question—quality vs. quantity.

What does that mean, quality vs. quantity? We all make this choice, every day really, about things that we perceive will improve the quality of our life at the expense of the quantity of our life (how long we will live). We do it with the foods we eat, whether or not to drink alcohol, smoke/chew tobacco, use/abuse prescription (and non-prescription) medications, use recreational drugs, engage in physical activity, and on and on and on. Sure, the impact is tiny, usually a drop in the bucket, but over time, slowly but surely, those drops add up, and then one day the doctor says, "you are pre-diabetic" or "your cholesterol is getting high," or any other number of warning statements, and we wonder how we got there. Then we make a choice, quality vs. quantity. We don't consciously do it, but we do it nonetheless. Quantity often means making a lifestyle change; quality means we keep doing what we are doing.

As a species, we gravitate toward quality, which is a here-and-now concept, as opposed to quantity, which is a down-the-line concept, until it's not. I had breast cancer. Who knows, maybe I still do. There is no test for it, I just have to sit and wait and see if something grows large enough to be detected. The good news is it takes a long time to grow, years really. The bad news is it takes a long time to grow, years really, so I get to sit and wait and wonder for years, or more. I have very real choices to make, right here and right now, that will impact my life, quality and quantity, with no guarantees.

Wouldn't it be nice if we had built-in calculators that told us how long we will live and how everything we do impacts our longevity? That if we eat that double cheeseburger with fries, it will shave two days off our life (hypothetical), and if we opt for the salad instead, we will live one day longer? We would have quantifiable data to work with, to make rational choices with. Maybe we are expected to live to be 104 years old and two days less doesn't matter that much to us. What if we are 69 years old and are expected to live to be 75 years old? Those two extra days suddenly carry more meaning. Only, we don't know. All we know is what doctors tell us about the hypothetical health impact of random items in general. In general, smoking is bad for you, fruits and vegetables are good. But if you are diabetic, fruit may not be all that good for you. As we get complicated, this general advice gets complicated. As we get complicated, the world gets more specific. So here I sit, post-breast cancer treatment, trying to get specific about the years ahead of me. Trying to add years where, in reality, none may even be subtracted.

And that's the rub. I don't know; none of us knows. We are all flying blind, making random choices based on what we hear, which is really living our lives based on the opinions of people far more credentialed than we are. Not a bad way to go, but enter the grain of salt. The human race is biased. Try as we might, we have no choice but to form an opinion and pick favorites. We take a side, root for a team, maybe vote for the underdog. We have been trained that way since our schoolyard days. So really, we are following the advice of potentially biased, more credentialed people than us. Also, not a bad thing, just something to be aware of.

So here I am, leaving the oasis of medical confidence to navigate the post-treatment world of real life all by my lonesome. Armed with my soy-free mantra, I am wondering how many years a person can really go without eating General Tso's Chicken (it's been a year!), and what difference it will make to the quantity of my life. I've given up the search for soy lecithin–free chocolate, and have settled for the mediocrity of Lay's Lightly Salted potato chips over the superior taste of Wise (there is no data on this, it is just my personal taste preference). One year out, I am still on board with these life choices, but as the years stretch on, maybe this mission I am on will fade away as the memory of my adventure with breast cancer fades ...

Who am I kidding? I have two half-moon scars emblazoned on my chest that say this memory will be with me for a long, long time.

Chapter 62 - Dr. Jekyll and Mr. Hyde

When I think about cancer, my mind goes into overdrive, ricocheting about in an effort to make sense of it. First it goes clinical, sterilizing the phenomenon into its most basic scientific facts. Science is cold, impartial, a potentially safe place to examine something that can kill you. Technically speaking, cancer is, at its core, damaged cells (nothing scary there) that are dividing unchecked (okay, just got scary). These cells no longer take direction from the body and divide on their own, doing as they please with no concern for the form they inhabit (closing in on terrifying). They have, in layman's terms, gone rogue. They are a part of us, but we no longer have any control. They have evolved from synergistic members of the team to inhospitable parasites with no thought but for their own agenda. Cancer is the Mr. Hyde to our Dr. Jekyll, and like Mr. Hyde, cancer is terrifying.

Maybe it is the whole out-of-control thing coupled with the no-reason-why thing and the no-definitive-treatment thing. Really, how can any treatment be a sure thing when there is no conclusive understanding or grasp of the cause? You can treat symptoms all day long, but unless you get to the root cause of something, you haven't cured a darn thing. Sure, there are theories as to why cancer grows, but for every person it is different, and what likely caused cancer to grow in one person does nothing in another under the same conditions. To me, these are scientific estimates of likelihood, more-likely-than-not scenarios and measured surmises of possibilities researchers hold to be true, until they find out they are not.

Don't get me wrong, for the record, I am grateful for the work of scientists all over the world who are looking for answers, I just take it with a grain of salt. In the end, they are trying to draw a straight line while riding on a merry-go-round. To me, and this is my opinion so take it with a grain of salt too, looking for the cure for symptoms doesn't address the cause. It's like plugging holes in a leaky dam with no concern for the water level that is causing the dam to spring leaks. That said, when the dam springs enough leaks, you really do have to address the leaks, which is where we likely are with cancer today, plugging leaks as fast as they spring up while trying to come up with a reason why they happen in the first place.

Like I said, my mind has a tendency to ricochet about. Once I've beaten the heck out of cancer clinically, I go fantastical. It is how I understand things best, to personify seemingly identity-less nemeses and give them personalities and a voice. It only seems fair that once I've listened to what science has to say I also listen to what the subject has to say. If we listen closely, everything has a story, sometimes hopeful, sometimes cautionary, so to me, it would behoove me to listen closely to what my breast cancer has to say. I don't want to miss the message the first time. Whatever it is, I don't need it repeated.

Louise L. Hay wrote an interesting reference guide to the inner voices of our ailments called *Heal Your Body A-Z*. In it, she talks about cancer in general as stemming from a deep hurt, a long-standing resentment, or a deep secret or grief that eats away at the self. Add breast issues to the mix and she points to a refusal to nourish the self, putting everyone else first, over-mothering, overprotection, an overbearing attitude. When I read that, it was like looking in a mirror. I felt like Dr. Jekyll must have when he got his first glimpse of Mr. Hyde. Kind of dark, I know, but if you would rather go the Disney princess route, then let's just say that this shoe fit better than Cinderella's. As a rule of thumb, I find that if a concept leaves me feeling gut-punched with an "oh crap" chaser, then it's likely that I'm onto something.

We all have baggage from our past. That's really just a cliché way of saying that I have experiences that didn't sit well, so I packed them away so I wouldn't have to think about them anymore. Quite often, these experiences happen when we are younger, or at a point in our lives when we didn't have the tools to process or understand them. Life events are much scarier when we are children, when everything seems bigger than life. The good news is I am an adult now. I can unpack those old events, revisit them from the safety of adulthood, and decide whether they really were as horrible as I thought they were. I usually find they are not. I also find that none of my baggage is my mother's fault, my father's fault or anyone else's fault. It is mine and mine alone, and, ironically, it made me who I am today (bet you didn't see that coming). Like it or not, it is the trials we face in life that mold us. They make us strong, give us the moxie to face down, say, cancer, and survive. They are also life's tests. Get them wrong and we get to redo them, over and over and over, until we do something different, until we get it right.

Breast cancer really does have a loud, booming voice. The gist of the message is, keep doing what you are doing, *I dare you.*

Chapter 63 - Just for Today

Just for today. It's a powerful statement. It makes me feel like I can do this, do anything, just for today. Tomorrow is another day and I will deal with that when it comes, but today, just for today, I can deal with this, whatever this is, that today will bring me.

When I was a child, my mother used to coax me through unpleasant situations with the saying, "This too shall pass." It worked. I could muddle through anything focused on the future, on a time when the unpleasantness would be behind me and life was rosy again. I carried this mantra into my adult years, propping myself up with it when the hopeful golden patina of the day gave way to a dowdy dull gray.

In the end, it served its purpose; time moved on, the day ended, and with it any unsettling chill faded into a whisper of memory. Somehow, though, I feel like I may have missed something, missed the point. In the end, if I am waiting for something to be over, if I am focused, however briefly, on tomorrow, the angst of the present moment glossed over, endured rather than engaged, then nothing is learned. Eyes on the horizon, the wonders of the sea at your feet are missed. Eyes on tomorrow, today really never happens at all.

When I was diagnosed with breast cancer in June of 2016, I made a conscious decision to live in the present. In my mind, my life depended on it, and in reality, it quite literally did. Every test result was a fork in the road; every decision committed me to a path. I firmly rooted myself in every moment of my treatment. I felt every prick, poke, and stab, physically and emotionally, examining them with more fervor than an entomologist does a rare bug. When I committed to chemotherapy, it was not a simple choice. It was researched and well thought out, not just the pros and cons of the treatment on the cancer, but the aftereffects on my life. The same with surgery. Yes, it was about removing the cancer, but it was also about preserving the function of my body. All through my breast cancer treatment, be it chemotherapy or surgery or radiation, I lived in the present. I may not have liked what was happening, but I was committed to the process, committed to the moment, committed to my life. For me, breast cancer will always be one of the most rewarding adventures of my life. That said, whatever lessons were to be learned, I definitely wanted to learn them the first time. No do-overs for this adventure.

I learned a lot in the sixteen months from breast cancer diagnosis to, well, now. I learned that -

- Life is scary, but not so scary that a couple of deep breaths and a hand to hold can't conquer.

My husband is my rock. His hand in mine is all I need to get through just about anything. He is not just my husband, though, he is my twin flame (think soul mate, but better!). I trust him to be there. A lot going on in that seemingly innocuous sentence—I trust him, and be there. Find someone, anyone, you *trust* and who will *be there*, and you can do pretty much anything.

- You don't find friends, they find you.

I met a lot of great people while I was in treatment. They found me, supported me, seemed to effortlessly know when to come forward and shrink back. Cancer treatment is a long, arduous journey. In many regards, we go through it alone, but if we take a leap of faith, the universe will sprinkle in exactly who we need when we need them.

- Cancer is as much about giving as it is about letting people give to you.

I learned how to be present for others from cancer, really present. To look past the facades of gaunt frames and tubes and see the bright shine in people's eyes that said, "I'm in here, and I'm alive!"

- Life happens in the moments you aren't paying attention to.

That's a fancy way of saying, life happens each and every second of each and every day. Live in those moments. Don't waste them planning for life to happen, because it's happening right now!

Lately, I have been trying too hard to be normal, to recapture who I was before breast cancer. I should read my own blog posts. Today is glorious! The air is crisp and the faint scent of burning leaves is drifting on vague currents of air. If I close my eyes, I can almost imagine fall, real fall, with orange and red and yellow leaves and the hope of snow. And if I open them, it is fall in Florida, and it is a glorious, glorious moment to be in.

Chapter 64 - Attitude Is Everything

Attitude is everything. I come back to it again and again, in my meditation, in my spiritual reading, in my daily life. I will even go so far as to say that attitude is all that separates me, and you, from a good day and a crappy day. The moment I roll out of bed in the morning, I make the decision that today will rock or today will rot. We all do. Most of the time we don't even realize we are doing it, charting our own paths to bliss or disaster, yet we are, and we do.

I think if we all knew how much weight our outlook brought to the table each day, we would give ours a little more attention. For me, in the past, I wore whatever mood jumped to the forefront when I got out of bed. A couple of aches and pains, I put on my cranky pants; too many deadlines piling up, maybe a Scrooge frown; bumper-to-bumper traffic on the way to work, I'm definitely giving Gru (*Despicable Me*) a run for his money. These are all choices, conscious choices. I can just as easily shake off the aches and pains and be grateful for the body I have, knowing full well that, just like every day, a little movement will limber things up and I'll be fine. Too many deadlines, no big deal. It won't be the first time and it won't be the last. I have thirty years of unmissed deadlines under my belt, this time will likely be no different. The same goes for traffic. Some days there is more, some days there is less, but traffic always is, so another option is to kick back with my favorite radio station and enjoy the impromptu leisurely ride.

Choices, people, we have choices! A funny thing happened when I started making different ones.

It started when I was diagnosed with breast cancer. Since I was neck deep in a life-changing event, I did some emotional housecleaning to declutter and destress. It wasn't that hard. Day to day things get really, really small when you have breast cancer. Deadlines? Off the radar; I had chemo to survive. Traffic? Whatever, I was just thrilled to still be part of the flow. Aches and pains? They were a fact of life. I woke up, I was alive, in my book it was the best day ever! Attitude, it was everything, and interestingly enough, that perspective has given me amazing insight into my current waning attitude.

So here I am, nine months post-chemo, eight months post-mastectomy and four months post-radiation, and my attitude, quite honestly, has begun to suck (harsh, maybe, but the occasional self-slap in the face can do wonders to get my head out of my ego). The aches and pains have begun to matter again, deadlines light a fuse, and traffic, don't get me started on the traffic. Some days I look in the mirror and I can swear I see Gru wearing cranky pants and a Scrooge cap. What happened? My attitude changed. I'm no longer in life-or-death mode, and regular life has reinstated itself to its prior level of inflated self-importance. Fortunately for me, I still have perspective.

My perspective is that it's just as easy to live life without the drama and hokum. Life can have deadlines and traffic and aches and pains without cranky pants and Gru and Scrooge. Mundane daily events are not inherently any better or any worse than any other events, we make them that way with … you guessed it, our attitudes! A little tweak, or attitude adjustment, as it were, and these events take on a whole new light.

So how does one adjust one's attitude? Me, I meditate every day. I find ten to twelve minutes of meditation when I wake up in the morning is the perfect elixir to start the day. With meditation, I can work out the mental and emotional kinks that tend to percolate overnight, the ones that turn every event into the straw that breaks the camel's back, and start the day with a clean slate.

Over the past eighteen months, I have found that when I meditate consistently, meaning every day, my interactions with people are better. I am more patient, work is less stressful, even my cat spends more time with me. When I don't meditate, my attitude starts to nosedive, and any number of moods can march out the door in the morning. For a mere ten minutes a day, I can enjoy the day rather than begrudge the day.

For me, it's a no-brainer. I like being unruffled, unstressed, relaxed (working on Zen) me.

Give yourself the gift of ten minutes. Sit, close your eyes, inhale slowly, exhale slowly, and let the magic begin.

For those that prefer to move, take a walk in nature, alone, a casual stroll, not a power walk, and absorb your surroundings. Listen to the sounds, smell the scents, look at the trees and plants and sky, and absorb the calm around you.

Start today.

Chapter 65 - Emotional Coal

Yesterday, in a post-Thanksgiving turkey-glazed-haze, I was mentally thumbing through the past year, the ups and downs and sideways moments that had come and gone and shaped my experience with breast cancer. That's what Thanksgiving is all about, right? Giving thanks for the blessings of the past year? Maybe it was the mashed potatoes talking, maybe it was the book on Kabbalah I am reading, but in that moment, the true gifts of the past year stepped forward and took a bow. I was not surprised by them. Honestly, I was more surprised that it took me this long to recognize them. You see, life's true gifts are not always the comfortable moments in life. The most meaningful gifts are more often the ones that make us squirm, the difficult, sometimes soul-crushing moments that test our mettle, and give us perspective.

For instance, for me, chemo was a wonderful adventure. I know, nuts, right? Once I made the choice to have chemo, there was no use griping about it, so I made the best of it and decided to find the nuggets of gold it had to offer. So I set aside the fact that poison was dripping into my vein, and of course the post chemo-day bodily havoc that would follow, and focused on the people and the pampering. I thought, at the time, that all the really nice nurses were the gift, with their lovely stories told while I snuggled under warm blankets, happily munching on warm cookies. I trusted them. I was happy and calm.

They were a gift, each and every one of them, but they were not THE gift. The true gift was the one nurse that rubbed me, and my husband, Ken, the wrong way. I can't recall her name, but she presided over my one unhappy, uncomfortable, anxiety-filled infusion. She rattled me, my cage and my perspective. The reality was, and is, chemo nurses are a crap shoot. For me, each week I had a new smiling face cruise-directing my treatment. My experience was in his or her hands. This one nurse, while I'm sure she meant well, she was the true "gift." She, unbeknownst to her, taught me that warm, comfortable infusions nestled in the bosom of trust and calm are a gift. She, my friends, was my black coal of perspective.

It is easy to be grateful for the happy moments in life, the smiles that light our way, the laughter that tickles our ear, but I say we should also be grateful for the less-amazing events. The losses that leave a void aching to be filled, the tears shed to wash away the pain etched on our cheeks, the anger that bubbles over for injustices, real and perceived. I am of the opinion, as are a long list of philosophers and gurus, that without sorrow we cannot know true joy, without lack we cannot appreciate abundance, and without pain we cannot truly appreciate pleasure. Without their counterparts, emotions ring hollow. They become bells with lackluster tones, heralding good fortune that no one bothers to notice anymore due to its unerring regularity. How much more melodious life would be if we listened with zeal and abandon to all the tones of the emotional scale, the ominous as well as the lilting, with equal openness and attention, embracing each in their turn for the range they bring and the perspective they offer.

I don't expect anyone to enjoy sad, frustrating, or anger-filled moments; I certainly don't. I do recognize what they bring to my life, though, and I do recognize that once I have identified them, I can work on changing them. Our emotions, like notes on a scale, are our own to play, as we wish. But I am getting off track. That, my friends, is for another week ... For now, suffice it to say that a little emotional coal may not be the gift you had hoped for, but in time you will find it to be the best gift you ever received.

Chapter 66 - Yup, I'm Still Insane

I've been wrestling with this feeling for the past few days, this gritty lump that's stuck in my craw and refuses to dislodge. I've meditated on it, yoga-ed on it, thought on it, frowned on it, yet there it sits, stuck there. Then, driving to work yesterday, it hit me, I'm still insane. Yup, genuinely certifiable. I meet the criteria. I've heard it scores of times over the years, you probably have too, that the definition of insanity is doing the same thing over and over and expecting a different result. Yet here I am, doing the same thing over and over and expecting a different outcome, and apparently now it's stuck in my craw.

That's what I get for thinking I've grown; too big for my britches is about all I've accomplished. If you want to get the universe's attention, turn your back, just for a second, and it will swat your bottom with a reality check faster than you can glance over your shoulder to see what's coming. So how did I get here, this escalating tête-à-tête with the cosmos? Simple really, I let the good opinion of other people get a toehold and worm in.

I like that phrase—the good opinion of other people. I heard Dr. Wayne Dyer say it in a lecture probably thirty years ago and it stuck with me. The gist is that other people's opinions are just that, their opinions. Ask one hundred people what they think about something, anything really, and you will get one hundred different *opinions*. That's right, *opinions*. They are the *good opinions* of other people. They are perfectly valid opinions, and I will go one step further and say they are also perfectly valid choices, for those people, but maybe not for me, or for you. What is right for me is what I think, what I like, and what, in the end, makes me happy, as it is for you. And here, my friends, is where I went awry, how I got into this mess with grit stuck in my craw. I let someone else's opinion cloud over my own.

To be clear here, sharing opinions is great, but like anything, we can take it too far. For instance, do you predicate your opinion of something, or someone, on what your friends, family, or coworkers think? I call that "opinion gathering," when you need to validate your own opinion before putting your own stamp of approval on it. The basic flaw with opinion gathering is that, at its core, it means you don't think your own opinion is good enough. How can that be? It is only good enough if it has been validated? (Pause and let that sink in.) It may feel safer to base your decisions on the consensus of your besties, but how on earth, my friend, do you get to be you under the weight of all those opinions? Sure, it's nice when someone weighs in that the bohemian look you were going for is really more early-American hobo, but in the end, the choice on whether to sally forth or alter course is still up to you, because all of it is just their opinion.

Okay, that was heavy. Back to me. So here I am, post-chemo, mastectomy and radiation, navigating the landscape of never-gonna-be-the-same and who-am-I-now, so I thought I'd have a little fun. Over Thanksgiving I had my toenails and fingernails painted purple with white polka dots. Why not, right? It's been a long time since I had nails that weren't threatening to detach from my fingers at the slightest provocation, so now that they are healthy and strong again, I decided to celebrate with gusto. It's sort of a throwback to when I was young and bold, when I did things for fun with a devil-may-care attitude and didn't give a hoot about offered opinions. And you know what? It felt great! Now, as my fingers dance across the keyboard, all I have to do is glance down to be reminded of the playfulness that is always there inside me just waiting for a chance to express itself, which brings me to the next bit.

With Christmas closing in, I've been thinking about a blog post I did back on April 13, 2017, (*Chapter 35 - Flat Blue Sky*), in which I daydreamed about a time when my hair had grown back and what sort of fun thing I could do with it to herald the second coming of my locks. I finally put that on the front burner and had some highlights done. Teal and purple; I love it!

And that should be all that matters, shouldn't it? That I love it? Then came the grit.

I won't say who delivered the grit, because who doesn't matter. Let's face it, there will always be people in our lives whose opinion will strike a chord. For me, the delicate area of self-expression that is always trying to cast off the gray trappings of life and splatter them with color is most vulnerable, for you maybe it is something else. Try as I might, some people's validation counts. Not in an it-will-change-my-opinion sort of way, but in a no-grit-in-my-craw sort of way. I feel like they didn't get the memo that there is a time to have an opinion and a time to just be happy for your friend (or family member, or whoever it is). So, since it seems I can't make their opinion not matter (yes, there is a time to admit defeat), I can spin the dial and change my own attitude about it all. A small (or large, depending on your grit level) change in perspective and voila! The annoying irritation is now a gift. Remember, without an irritant there is no opportunity for growth or change, which is what I have now, an opportunity to break the chains of insanity, to change the narrative, to do something different.

Then again, that's just my opinion.

Chapter 67 - An Angel's Kiss

I'm not going to lament the sudden drop in temperature that reminds me that Central Florida is not like its perpetually sunbaked sister to the south. In reality, it is this annual reminder that the rest of the United States has seasons that attracts me to this region. Now, before real confusion sets in, a reminder that seasons exist is not a claim to actually have seasons. For instance, Monday morning it was thirty-eight degrees; by noon it was sixty. A few days later it was back in the seventies and next week we will be closing in on eighty degrees, relegating cool weather to nothing more than a wistful hope.

To enjoy the peek-a-boo cool weather, you have to act fast. Monday night, I lit a fire in the fireplace and entertained a fantasy that a white Christmas could be possible; lo and behold, the next morning the front lawn was blanketed with a white-ish sheen, courtesy of frost. That's as close as I'm going to get, barring some behind-the-scenes negotiation between the Heat Miser and his brother, the Snow Miser. Snow and frost aside, what I love about this time of year is that undefinable something that clings to the air and makes me feel like anything is possible. Yes, that's right, that sappy, schmaltzy Hallmark Christmas movie-esque feel that everyday occurrences are indeed miracles unto themselves and everything is just as it should be.

I have been struggling lately with the push-me-pull-you tango going on between work me and take-care-of-myself me. After my cancer diagnosis, I spent a lot of time soul searching, which resulted in a concerted effort to disentangle myself from the constraints of the "norm" so I could create a safe haven of normalcy for myself within which to heal. That may seem incongruous, to reject the "norm" to create normalcy, but for me, an existence that includes a 24/7 bombardment of news, emails, texts, and phone calls is anything but normal. I'm not going say it's not normal for anybody, because there is an entire generation growing up that doesn't know anything different. They will have to navigate their own idea of normalcy. For me, information overload is anything but normal, which is why I opted to pull the proverbial plug and wipe the slate clean so I could fashion an existence for myself that nurtured my soul, not nagged it. Now, post treatment, as I ease back into the rapids of regular life, I find the mud of the "norm" sucking at my boots again, threatening to drag me into the current to swim with the rest of the salmon. And then I was kissed by an angel.

Have you ever been kissed on the forehead by an angel? I was, last night. It's the strangest thing, to have ethereal lips press ever so softly against your forehead, the faintest wisps of gossamer hair brushing your cheek as she (or he) leans over to deliver their blessing. "Everything is as it should be," washes over you, definitive and undeniable. Yes, everything is exactly as it should be.

And so there you have it. Life is a process, a slow, steady march on a turning, twisting, winding road. Each perfect point in time on that road has no judgement, no irreverence, because it knows how perfect, how unique it is, while at the same time remains humbled by the endless points of time just like it that are equally as perfect and unique. My hope is to one day be able to revel in each point in time in each day I am blessed by, to see every moment as the gift it is and each experience as a miraculous thread that connects me to the universe, full of hope and promise and opportunity. First, though, I have to deal with the mud sucking at my boots. Apparently, it too is exactly as it should be.

Chapter 68 - Life's like That

Last Saturday, I pulled all my dresses out of the closet and put them on, one by one, to see how they fit my new physique. Let's face it, my torso is crafted somewhat differently now. A double mastectomy will do that for you. I was somewhat surprised to find that dresses I never thought would be passable fit great and some that I thought for sure would be keepers are headed for the thrift store. Life's like that, full of little surprises.

Me being me, I can never just let something like that go. It intrigued me, the various ways that exercise could have played out. It is a very different scenario to shop in a store for clothes when you have no breasts than to try on your own dresses, one at a time, dresses that pre-surgery looked fabulous (why else would I have bought them?) and now have the potential to hammer home the obvious, again and again and again. Yet nothing happened. No mood swing into the Netherlands, no reflection staring back encouraging self-doubt; just an incongruous happiness and feeling of freedom.

I am still baffled that not having breasts doesn't bother me. There I was, trying on dress after dress, and all I could think about was that they looked better now than when the girls were trapped in there longing for freedom. The dresses that didn't work I considered taking to a seamstress to take in the chest area, but decided I didn't like them enough to make the investment.

Still, fit or not, it turned out to be great fun shopping in my own closet, each familiar dress unveiled as a potential new look and actually turning out to be just that, a brand new look for me. As a bonus, dresses I hadn't worn in years, because I didn't have the right bra, were no longer a problem. No more bra straps showing, no more side body flesh smooshed up into unnatural contours that none of us has when we're not trussed up in a brassiere. Now, everything sits as it should, no fuss or muss. Clothes fit or they don't, without consideration for the correct holsters for the ladies. No cramming or squashing or squeezing. Me and the dress, that's it.

The women out there know what I'm talking about. I've never met a bra I really liked, and when you do finally find one that fits, it is guaranteed to wear out in three to four months and you'll need a new one. By that time, the company that makes it will either have discontinued it or made enough changes to it that it's unrecognizable and unwearable. Sure, we all flip longingly through the Victoria's Secret catalogs, but my profession does not include sitting still in my underwear for a camera with most of my breast strategically on display, so let's be realistic on that front. If you want what she's wearing, be prepared to be sporting some serious cleavage. It is a great look for date night with your spouse, but not so great a look for the office.

Can you tell I love the new me? Granted, life threw lemons at me, so I'm making gallons of lemonade, but consider it. What would life be like without the trappings of convention? Without the requirement of a breast code that ensures we fit into the social circle we have been thrown into? Me, I swim along with everyone else without a sideways glance. I feel like I'm the lucky winner of some sort of free breast pass. It's kind of cool, if I do say so myself.

Okay, before I sign off, I want to remind everyone, attitude is everything. I think my free pass comes from the fact that I have given myself a free pass. I neither call attention to nor detract from the changes in my physique. Honestly, I don't give them a second thought. I am wearing the same wardrobe pre- and post-mastectomy with the exception of a bag of bras I couldn't donate to Goodwill fast enough. My clothes are an expression of the joy I feel to be blessed to hitch a ride in this body for this life. Are yours?

Chapter 69 - A Patient Observer

Two slices of raisin bread, toasted, with some fruit on the side. Honeydew melon these days, it changes with the seasons. As I buttered my toast this morning, it came to me that all during chemotherapy I made my own raisin bread. Now I buy it at the store—Dave's Killer Raisin Bread. It also occurred to me that there was a time, pre-cancer, when I would have expended a good deal of energy chastising myself for turning to store-bought bread in lieu of baking my own. Now, I just notice. I notice the change in my routine like I notice the change in the clouds, as a patient observer. There is no judgement, no discontent, no self-punishment. I have meditation to thank for that.

I have a cold. I've tried to wrap my head around some sort of meaning behind it, but there doesn't seem to be any. It's just a cold. Quite different from the last cold I had. It was a little over a year ago, Thanksgiving 2016 to be exact. I remember it clearly because I was in the middle of my first phase of chemo, the part that kills off your white blood cells along with everything else, and I had caught a cold. It frightened me, because in my mind the common cold I had could kill me. That is the cancer horror story I had managed to find and read, where someone finishes their chemo, is cancer-free and is taken down by a cold. Drat. It was the only word that came to mind. Drat.

This cold is quite different. I have a fully functioning immune system and death is not at the table. It's just a cold, or maybe a mild flu, and I'm just observing. The aches and pains that come with a cold, the runny nose and stuffy head. If all else fails, a fever will set in and cook the germs where they hide. It's fascinating really, the body's elegant response to drive off invaders. I don't interfere; I just let my body do its thing. No Tylenol or Nyquil or Vicks VapoRub or heating pads, just my good old-fashioned immune system, Vitamin C Bio Fizz, and chicken. I eat what I crave and it seems this cold calls for chicken. How do I know? I listen to my body. Meditation will do that for you.

So what does it mean, to be an observer? To me, it means to take a step back and take in the whole picture, rather than be invested in the fray. I try to be in the moment, not of the moment. For example, being in traffic, or simply driving with other people on the road, is a challenge for many people. Other drivers go too fast or too slow, change lanes erratically, run yellow (and red) lights, and on and on and on. The bottom line—they exist. How dare they! I say, so what? If I'm in the slow lane doing my thing and someone hurtles by me one lane over, why should I care? Most likely it is not because of my deep concern for their welfare and that they might get a ticket. No, usually it is because they have violated some imaginary rule I created and so I experience a feeling of being personally wronged. Crazy, right? Really, there should be absolutely no reason why I react at all, why any of us do, yet we do. We can't help ourselves. And so I meditate.

Driving the three hours to my mother's house last Saturday, I was pleasantly surprised by my lack of interest in or reaction to the antics of other drivers. I just let them do their thing and I did mine. And oddly enough, without the gyrations of jockeying for position and lane changing and such, I arrived in two and a half hours instead of three.

I'm baffled by that part. I didn't go any faster than normal; I just drove in the slow lane and minded my own business. Maybe it's some sort of cosmic reward, positive reinforcement for good behavior. It does make some sense, because when I used to worry about being late for things, I usually was. Now, I give myself the appropriate amount of travel time and, traffic or not, I always make it on time, even when bumper-to-bumper traffic threatens to derail me. I just take a deep breath, let it all go, and trust that it will all work out as it should, and it does.

Funny thing about that, if you trust that everything will work out as it should, it always will. I mean, how else could anything possibly work out, except as it is meant to? Meditation doesn't hurt, either.

Chapter 70 - A Haircut like That

Lately, I keep hearing reference to "I had a haircut like that once." The haircut that doesn't need scissors; the one where your hair just falls out in clumps, then sticks to you as though hanging on for dear life. It doesn't want to go, really it doesn't, but its roots have failed, so each strand ups its static-electric game in a vain attempt to latch on to some other part of you, delaying the inevitable for as long as possible.

I remember getting in the shower and running my fingers through my hair. Silly me, I thought I could just rinse out the loose strands. Large clumps of hair came away, clinging to my fingers. It was like petting my cat in the spring, or for you dog lovers, like trying to brush the winter coat out of a Husky or Samoyed. The hair just kept coming and coming. And it sticks to you, for all it's worth, in one last-ditch effort to avoid becoming the lining of a bird's or squirrel's nest, or worse, of fulfilling its dust-to-dust circle of life march much sooner than intended. It's really hard to wash hair off yourself when it keeps falling out. You end up a human chia-pet, but with hair. Those were good times (*Chapter 5 - Hair, Hair, Hair or Not*). Really, they were. I can say that because it never occurred to me that my hair would not grow back.

It should, you know, grow back (if you are wondering). I miss my post-chemo curly fuzz. I felt like a baby chick. My husband couldn't resist rubbing my downy-soft head, nor could I. Now it is back to normal; thick, soft in a coarse kind of way, peppered with gray (less than before chemo, so thanks for that), and now streaked with teal and purple (not thanks to chemo, thanks to Jeffrey).

I saw a woman at the grocery store yesterday with "a haircut like that." I stopped to chat, opening by asking how she was doing. She looked puzzled, so I offered, "I had a haircut like that once." Those are powerful words, a passcode to a not-so-secret club. She softened and we chatted about treatments we had, losing our hair and getting it back, and eyebrows. Her hair is coming back and her head itches (your head itches when your hair falls out and itches when it grows back in). She is sad that it is coming in a little grayer, but she is in the chemo-fuzz faze. Maybe it will get darker when her real hair comes back. She was afraid it wouldn't grow back at all, so she has that. Her eyebrows are coming in thicker than they were before, so she has that too.

Then we touched on hospitals and she changed. I don't recall where she said she was treated (it was local, but nowhere I recognized), but she suddenly looked bullied and worn out. She wished she had gotten a second opinion before treatment, but she was frightened and just wanted it over with. I can understand that; it was my first instinct too. I just wanted the tumor out. Thank God for doctors with really, really bad bedside manner, or I might have gone with the flow too. She also had reconstruction done, which she is now second-guessing. It is a long healing process and she's likely not done with it physically, but she seemed really over it mentally and emotionally. The longer the conversation went on, the sadder she became. That was not my intention, and I couldn't see any way to make her feel better, so I wished her well and we both moved on.

As I walked away, I almost felt guilty for my year of pampering and happy-with-my-choices attitude. Almost, but not quite, because it made me realize how important one voice can be. For me, it was my mother's voice. My mother always got a second opinion if she didn't like the answer the doctor gave her; she still does. Heck, she gets another opinion on just about everything. It served me well. For me, it isn't exactly about getting another opinion, it is about finding a doctor, or mechanic, or teacher, or anyone that is going to provide a service for me, that resonates with me, and I can only do that by getting a second, or third, opinion when the first ones leave me confused, sad, or both.

We all deserve to interact with providers who can explain things in a way that we understand, that will take the time to patiently walk us through things until we are comfortable and ready to proceed. I am blessed to have found a team of doctors that understood me and what my goals were. It was no accident, I called the new patient desk at Orlando Health and told them about who I am, and they matched me with a doctor that resonated with my personality. Still, it was not an easy process. I met with an oncologist, Dr. Regan Rostorfer, who I adore. Then I met with a surgeon, radiation oncologist, and plastic surgeon. Only the surgeon made the cut— Dr. Jeffrey Smith. The other two I continued to interview for. The plastic surgeon became moot, as I elected not to have reconstruction, but I still met with a wonderful plastic surgeon in Winter Park who explained in depth every reconstructive procedure, which was instrumental in my decision to forgo reconstructive surgery. I eventually found an awesome radiation oncologist, Dr. Tomas Dvorak, who explained the nuances of the various types of radiation treatment, how they work, the possible side effects and possible impact to each layer of tissue in its path. It was fascinating and encouraging, and gave me the peace of mind I needed to make a decision and move ahead with a positive, hopeful attitude.

I am grateful for the woman in the grocery store. She reminded me of the gift of choice. We all have it. It is difficult to choose service providers, but I see first meetings as interviews. They get to meet me; I get to meet them. Then they get to examine the problem and tell me what they think, and that part is pretty much pass fail. If I walk away shell-shocked or uncomfortable, they have failed, and I move on. Even the worst of news can be done with grace and someone can walk away feeling okay. This applies to everything we do. I am baffled by the stories I hear about folks who get their car fixed by mechanics they don't trust and are convinced they are being deceived. Or people who don't like their doctors, yet they go to them year after year. Choices, people, you have choices!

The woman in the grocery store also reminded me of the choices I have ahead of me. As the course of my breast cancer changes from treatment to follow-up visits, so shall the course of this blog. My humorous anecdotes about chemotherapy and radiation are a thing of the past. No more blow-by-blow accounts of mastectomies or port surgeries. What stretches ahead are (hopefully) very mundane follow-up visits. Five years of them, to be exact. First on the agenda is a bone-density scan next week. Stay tuned for that, I'm sure it will be a hoot and a half!

By the way, thanks to all of you for following and sharing my blog. Writing this blog was cathartic for me these past fifteen months, and that so many people made the choice to read and share it means a lot.

Chapter 71 - Letting Go of Fear

I had my six-month follow-up visit with my radiation oncologist last week. It's hard to believe that it has been six months since my last radiation treatment, which means it has been ten months since my last chemotherapy treatment. I got the "all clear" yesterday, but it felt hollow. The follow-up for double mastectomy patients seems too simplistic, too fraught with the potential for error. Really, all he did was ask me how I felt and then palpate (fancy word for knead and poke) at my chest and underarm, looking for irregularities, sore spots, anything that could mean something nefarious. It's hard to tell, at least for me, although he seemed very sure, that it's all clear.

My left underarm is a mass of dense scar tissue, which at any given moment is in various stages of being sore (due to my vigorous stretching) and being lumpy (due to it trying to bind up again). I do my own self-check every couple of weeks, but all I feel is dense, lumpy tissue. My oncologist, Dr. Regan Rostorfer, gave me a tutorial on what scar tissue feels like the last time I saw him. I would point out what I thought felt like possible lumps in the dense tissue and he would shoot it down, telling me it's just scarring, that it felt perfectly normal. Not ideal by any means, but it helped. Now I no longer get a clenching in my stomach when I knead at my scarring. The truth is, it all feels the same, like a shifting, fibrous area of healing-tearing-then-healing scar tissue. Perfectly normal, and so, all clear.

The most frightening part of a breast cancer diagnosis, and I suspect any cancer diagnosis, is the unknown. You spend months (at least I did) getting tested to narrow down the scope of the cancer, all with no definitive answers. Then you spend months in treatment (chemotherapy in my case) hoping the cancer will respond, with no definitive answers. Then you have surgery, where you get some answers, but as it was in my case, the caveat of door number three, behind which there are more questions than answers.

229

Then more treatment (radiation), after which you are put on a wait-check-and-see protocol to make sure nothing appears again. So now, after the frightening part of my breast cancer diagnosis and treatment has subsided and is a thing of the past, and the happy-go-lucky giddiness of treatment-free days is waving its hand frantically in the air for a turn, the new frightening thing about breast cancer is waiting to see if it comes back.

To me, fear is like playing a rigged game of Jumanji. No matter what you do, your situation is destined to keep getting worse. I say, let it go. Fear can be paralytic, stymieing your every move until your world gets smaller and smaller and all the pleasure is sucked out of life. Yes, sometimes bad things happen, but a lot more often they don't. For every horrible end result I can think of (and trust me, I can think of A LOT), there are exponentially more good outcomes to the same scenario. In the end, you just have to trust that it is not your time yet; you just have to let it all go.

And so it is with breast cancer follow-up. For someone who has lived her life being afraid of everything and trying to mitigate and control the outcome of every scenario (it's safer that way), that was one tough lesson. I spent the first fifty-five years of my life being afraid of what horrible thing could befall me in the course of everyday activities, and yet here I sit, staring in the lion's mouth, day in and day out, and I'm not afraid at all. When I look back at the lifetime I spent not doing things because of the specter of fear that hovered over me, tapping me on the shoulder to point out all the darkest possibilities of life that could befall me, I shake my head at the pointlessness of it all.

Yes, that's right, the pointlessness of it. Whenever we act out of fear, the outcome is pointless. There was a time when fear served its purpose, when it kept us from becoming dinner for something higher on the food chain, but no more. Now, with nothing better to do with our fear response, we make stuff up to give it something to do, escalating everyday innocuous events into live-or-die situations. In the end, anything and everything could potentially cause your untimely demise, but most likely it won't. It's just the way it goes. But I guarantee you that if you spend all your time not doing things because they might kill you, then eventually something else will. Personally, from where I currently sit, a long life spent denying myself is a far worse fate than a potentially shorter one spent with a wicked grin on my face and satisfaction in my soul.

Before you queue up for bungee jumping or spelunking, not every soul is satisfied by the same adventures. Adventures don't have to be physically dangerous in nature. Emotional risks can be equally as terrifying. Whatever it is you have always wanted to do and followed up the thought with "I can't," that's your ticket to paradise. In the end, you may not even enjoy it, but the point is you tried, and that, my friends, is where the freedom, and the fun, is.

Chapter 72 - One Velvety Paw

My cat has developed a new routine. Yes, she still sleeps with me, curled in the crook of my arm so she can take full advantage of my body heat and a free hand to methodically stroke her until she drifts off to sleep on a cloud of kitty ecstasy. I know this because, in return, I get to fall asleep to her rhythmic purring. She sneaks away sometime in the night to do whatever it is that cats do in the middle of the night (no doubt up to no good. As most adults will attest, nothing good happens after midnight). She comes back around 5:30 a.m., before the alarm goes off, which she is not a fan of, to check up on me and get in some last-minute loving.

Normally she just barges in, leaping onto the bed with gymnastic-quality aplomb and then sauntering about, on the bed and on me, until I wake up. As of late she has adopted a new tactic. She leaps onto the bed (same gymnastic-quality aplomb), then makes her way carefully to my head and sits down to study me for a while.

There is something about the feline gaze. The laser focus of intent in their eyes can effortlessly reach into the depths of your brain and soul and will you awake. It is as if they have reached into your brain and flicked your on switch. It's not a jarring awakening, at least not for me, but rather a sudden realization that I've been summoned. Then, once I'm awake, she places one velvety paw on my shoulder as if to say, it will be all right.

One velvety paw. There is so much packed into that simple gesture, yet I really have no clue what she is trying to tell me. I did turn to the Internet, and a quick search revealed that touching with a paw is a sign of affection for cats. Then again, so is head butting. It feels like a kitty catch-all to me; if your cat isn't pissed off, it must be affection. No, I think it's something else, I'm just not sure what.

And so it is with relationships. When two people speak the same language, it is complicated; when you speak different languages and one of you is a cat, the difficulty meter goes off the charts. Imagine, though, a relationship where logically you should both be perfectly in sync, yet for the most part you are nearly always clueless. And so it is with me and my body. I think I know what's going on, what will inch me back to peak health and what will send me astray, but I really don't. What worked before cancer doesn't work now, and foods I would never have considered eating before are main staples now. It's all catawampus. I can't help but frown at how foreign my own body is to me, what makes it tick, sends it off-kilter. The reality, though, is we live in an ecosystem (our body) that exists in an ecosystem (the earth) that resides in the universe, and anywhere in all that something can happen to throw all the rest off-kilter and change the rules. I mean *really* change the rules.

And so it goes. Breast cancer was a game changer; two bouts of flu (albeit mild ones) in as many months is also a game changer. The paradigm I once lived in is gone. It died a slow, agonizing, horrible death (okay, I was depressed for half a day). Things change, and so I must continue to change with them. Like the proverbial tree in the wind, I must learn to bend (even more) and sway (even more) as each new challenge presents itself, leaving whatever bag of tricks and homespun user's guide I was using behind in favor of fresh ideas and a new normal.

Ah, I sound tired even to myself. Maybe it is post-flu malaise. One velvety paw; sometimes that is all we need. One brief touch of reassurance. Cats are rarely wrong, at least not my cat, and this time I'm sure she is right. It will be all right. It will continue to be an adventure, for sure, but it will definitely be all right.

Chapter 73 - Why You Need a Sacred Space

I never really understood the big deal behind sacred space. When I did my yoga training, the teacher recommended we each build personal altars. I dutifully searched the Internet to find examples of what mine should look like, completely missing the point. Flummoxed, I never did it. Even if I had built one, then what? The truth of the matter was, I had no idea what to do with an altar or how to create a sacred space. Then I got cancer.

It's interesting who you turn to and what you do when your head is spinning and you need something solid to hold on to. Me, I turned to the most capable person I know, someone I trusted and knew I could rely on. I turned to me. And what I needed at that point to be able to function was to clear my head. I needed a sacred space, so I built an altar.

An altar need not be fancy, or perfect. Mine is a low table, like for eating breakfast in bed. It sits on the floor in front of the picture window in our yoga room so I can sit cross-legged in front of it and enjoy the outdoors. The birds flit around the plants outside that window, and there is a hawk that uses the light pole as a lookout for his next move. It is an actively serene spot, one where life happens right outside and I can be an unobtrusive observer. It mimics what happens during meditation.

My altar-top is garnished with special objects that encourage feelings of comfort and safety. The unity candle from my wedding (what better day will there ever be than the day I said "I do" to my angel, Ken), a photo of my father and I, photos of Ken and I taken in a photo booth while we were dating, and a shallow bowl of stones I have collected from beaches and riverbanks with a beeswax tealight set in the center. When I sit with these items, the flame of the candle flickering over them, I am taken back to a simpler time, purer time, before-cancer time.

I meditate in front of my altar. It holds an energy that warms my body and connects me to the universe in ways that other places do not, cannot. I don't know the science behind it, nor do I care. There was a time when I would have analyzed the heck out of it, the psychology and physiology of it, but in reality the power of the mind, body, and spirit combined transcend what we understand about ourselves at this stage of our existence, and so some things I just accept as knowing. I don't need to go on faith on this one. I need only meditate in the glow of the candlelight.

In reality, we are our own sacred space. Even if we don't feel like we are, deep down inside is still that kernel of untouchable truth, the divinity within each of us. I realized early on that my job was to nurture and grow that small, neglected part of myself; to fan the small ember to a roaring flame that can withstand the howling winds of life.

As I grow stronger, with cancer treatment behind me and the day-to-day business of living at hand, it is becoming all too easy to neglect my tiny altar. Truth be told, I need more, a larger space to call my own, a place where my inner flame can explore at will. And so I am creating a new sacred space, a place where I can write, paint, think, be. In it I am surrounding myself with objects that have influenced my life and nurtured my soul. It is a combination of the ordered structure of an office and the chaotic melee of creativity. It is me.

I still have my tiny altar as well. It is where I dig deep, connect to the elusive inner me that often scuttles ahead of my understanding in an esoteric game of cat-and-mouse. I think it is time to change out some of the objects, or add others to the clutter. Maybe the new photo booth strip taken during chemotherapy? My bald head glowing like the alien girl in the movie, *Cocoon*. Those were special times. Sometimes, all it takes is a quiet moment of reflection with a favorite photo to realize that. One day, today will be one of those special times, a memory I look back upon with fondness. Why wait? I think I will start relishing this moment today.

Chapter 74 - Oh, What a Glorious Morning

Some days it's hard to feel grateful. Why is that? My life has not changed dramatically since yesterday. Granted, today is Sunday, which makes tomorrow Monday, as opposed to yesterday, which was Saturday with the promise of Sunday still on the horizon. I enjoy my job and do not have Monday doldrums, so the days of the week should not matter. Sure, I'd rather stay home and putter around the house any given day of the week, but my husband goes to work, so it would be lackluster puttering at best. It's always more fun when he's around. We don't have to be doing the same thing, or even be in the same room. Having his warm presence permeating the house is enough. The same with my kitty. Knowing she is sleeping somewhere in the house, her face free of fear or concern, is enough for me.

And so it is with gratitude. It is a see-saw ride, as I suspect it is with you. Some days I am bursting with thanks for all the blessings in my life, big and small. They parade before me in a conga line of blissful thoughts, each taking their bow in turn as I shower them with thanks. I couldn't forget about them if I tried. Other days, a milky cloud moves in and obscures the obvious, leaving me to flounder for even one grateful reflection. Like happiness, gratitude is not a given in life. It has to be worked at. Feeling grateful is as much an effort as not feeling grateful, so when gratitude eludes me, I make the effort to give the see-saw a push, back to a place where gratitude comes more naturally.

An easy path to gratitude for me is to look back over my adventure with breast cancer. I survived! Surviving breast cancer treatment comes to mind more often than one would think. There are dozens of ways that adventure could have gone south, and that's before even taking cancer into account. I went through chemotherapy, a double mastectomy, and radiation therapy, and I'm still standing. I'm very, very, super, uber grateful for that.

Then there's me in the aftermath. I feel great and I look pretty darn good flat. I feel comfortable, natural, attractive. My husband finds me attractive. I am the love of his life, as he is mine. No physical blemish can diminish that for either of us. I'm pretty darn grateful for that, too.

Then there are clouds. What is life without a peek at the clouds from time to time? They sashay across the sky in a Rorschach test of white blobs. If there is ever a way to turn the tide of gloom, it's a session with the sky. No matter what the outcome, delving into my psyche to chase the meaning of fluffy cloud images is always a hoot of a time. I've seen a menagerie of animals parade across the Florida sky over my backyard, as well as the occasional knight, gnome, and superhero, and they always leave me with a grin on my face and joy in my soul.

Bird songs are another fan favorite for me for seeking gratitude. The nuances of the songs bandied back and forth pull me out of myself, switching my attention from somber internal notes to the flighty whimsy of my feathered neighbors. I wonder what they say with their happy songs? Are they looking for a mate, sharing information on a tasty treat, or maybe just celebrating the day? I think they celebrate the day more than we think. They open their eyes to the rising sun, maybe the warm rays on their feathers nudging them awake, and burst into song, the bird version of "Oh, What a Beautiful Morning." It's hard not to sing right along with them!

Then again, I'm a morning person. My husband stares in wonder at the stars. They don't move me the same way, but I'm learning. Maybe it's because I like the here and now and the twinkle of the star I see happened thousands of years ago, or longer. I know, I am seeing the light now, but somehow to me it doesn't quite feel like the present moment.

So, here's an interesting notion, I actually burst into being in the past just like the star. We are both a culmination of the events that got us here, to this point in time, when the pinpoint of light that is the star completed its billions-of-miles journey, taking thousands of years, and I completed the fifty-sixth year-of-my-life journey and decided (realistically, at the urging of my husband) to tip my chin up to gaze at the stars, and we met, that star and I.

When I put it that way, it is pretty darn cool. I guess it's time to spend some time outside at night and expand my gratitude horizon. It is just an attitude, you know. What you are not grateful for today you can turn into a blessing with just a thought. Give it a try. For example, I'm grateful, in many ways, for my breast cancer. I have grown more as a person, become a better wife, friend, and daughter, and learned to appreciate the gifts in my life more as a result of a disease I chose to call an adventure, and that is one heck of a thing to be grateful for.

Now it's your turn. Turn your lemons into lemonade!

Notes

ABOUT THE AUTHOR

Juliana Steele lives in Central Florida with her husband, Ken, and their cat, Jill. She continues to write about life on her blog, Eudemonics.lol - How to Navigate Life When You Are Handed a Bucket of Lemons.

53722172R00142

Made in the USA
San Bernardino, CA
15 September 2019